St. Augustine Answers 101 Questions on Prayer

St. Augustine

St. Augustine Answers 101 Questions on Prayer

Compiled and edited by
Fr. Cliff Ermatinger

SOPHIA INSTITUTE PRESS®
Manchester, New Hampshire

Printed in the United States of America

Cover design by Theodore Schluenderfritz

On the cover: *St. Augustine in His Cell*, by Sandro Botticelli, Galleria degli Uffizi, Florence, Italy / The Bridgeman Art Library.

Sophia Institute Press®
Box 5284, Manchester, NH 03108
1-800-888-9344
www.sophiainstitute.com

Library of Congress Cataloging-in-Publication Data

Augustine, Saint, Bishop of Hippo.
St. Augustine answers 101 questions on prayer / [compiled by] Cliff Ermatinger.
p. cm.
Includes bibliographical references.
ISBN 978-1-933184-60-9 (pbk. : alk. paper) 1. Prayer — Christianity — Miscellanea. I. Ermatinger, Cliff. II. Title. III. Title: St. Augustine answers one hundred and one questions on prayer. IV. Title: St. Augustine answers one hundred one questions on prayer.
BV210.3.A925 2009
248.3′2 — dc22

2009027134

09 10 11 12 13 14 9 8 7 6 5 4 3 2 1

This book is dedicated to my mother,
who taught me to love talking with God.

∞

This book would not have been possible
without the resources and inspiration
provided by Fr. Agostino Trapé OSA.
His work introduced me to St. Augustine, and
his contagious love for St. Augustine infected
me and motivated me to write this book.
Grazie, Padre.

Contents

SEEKING GOD IN PRAYER

FINDING GOD IN PRAYER

PRAYER AND CONVERSION

PRAYER AND GRACE

PRAYER AND SALVATION

EFFECTIVE PRAYER

WHAT TO ASK FOR

WHAT NOT TO ASK FOR

PRAYING ALWAYS

CHRIST'S ROLE IN OUR PRAYER

For everything exterior is driven in this direction and that by the world's storms and tribulations. But there is a hermitage within, and there let us examine our faith . . . there where no man can see is this hermitage, where in hope we rest, as all troubles pass it by.

Sermon 47, 14, 23

∞

All our striving in this life consists in healing the eye of the heart in order to see God.

Sermon 88, 5

Introduction

"Where is God to be sought?"

"Is he to be sought even though he has been found?"

"If he knows what we need, why does God want us to ask him for what we need?"

"Do we attempt to change God's will when we ask him for things?"

Such were the questions that perplexed a young North African man who, in spite of his brilliant intellect and tenacious will, found no satisfying answers. The answer lay somewhere beyond human nature's most privileged gifts. Augustine Aurelius found the answers to these questions and many more, not through a mere accumulation of data, but ultimately through the experiential knowledge that accompanies an authentic encounter with Christ. This is what St. Paul means when he describes what it is to *comprehend with all the holy ones what is the breadth and length and height and depth, and to know the love of Christ that surpasses knowledge* (Eph. 3:18-19).

St. Augustine's writings continuously return to this experiential element of the relationship with God, in which he says, "spiritually to touch God a little is a great joy; but to grasp him is entirely impossible."[1] This experience bears within itself a certain healthy tension. We touch God but cannot grasp him; we know him, but he eludes our understanding. No matter; "it is better to find God without understanding him, than to understand him without finding him."[2]

It all brings about a burning desire that Augustine defines simply as "prayer."

To understand prayer, according to Augustine, we have to understand what it is to long for God.

Prayer and desire: for the Bishop of Hippo, these are interchangeable terms. Desire is what ensures prayer's interiority, thus saving it from becoming mindless repetition or pagan babbling (cf. Matt. 6:7). Upon desiring God we begin to possess him. Our longing for *that which no eye has seen, nor ear heard, nor has it ever entered into the heart of man* (cf. 1 Cor. 2:9), brings us to him whom we have desired with our whole being. Under God's grace, this search begins to shape our entire existence with faith, hope, and love — and leads us ever deeper into the desire for him.

∞

Much like the young Augustine, we all have some questions about prayer. But, unlike Augustine, most of us seldom come up with our own cogent and convincing answers. The purpose of this little book is to attempt to answer many of the most frequently asked questions I have met in my twenty-plus years of religious life. When confronted with such perplexing questions, I found that, in many cases, the Church Fathers offered a treasury of profound and beautiful solutions. And from amongst the many excellent patristic sources, Augustine increasingly claimed first place, owing to his practical counsels expressed in accessible language.

That's all fine for a quick reference. The only difficulty is that quite often his works do not purport to offer a systematic and complete study of any one topic. Such an approach would come later with the advent of Scholasticism, thanks in great part to that giant of the High Middle Ages, St. Thomas Aquinas.

To obtain a complete picture of what St. Augustine thought about any one topic, one has to read just about everything he ever wrote. That wouldn't be so problematic if he hadn't written more in his seventy-six years of life than most people will ever read in an equally long lifetime. To take our topic, for example, he never wrote a treatise on prayer or developed a formal theology of prayer. The closest he ever came to such an endeavor is his gem of spirituality, *Letter* 130, in which he counsels the widow Proba on the ways of prayer. With this modest book I seek to go beyond the contents of *Letter* 130 and bring to the reader the breadth of Augustine's reflections on prayer collected from over two hundred sources.

Perhaps a word of caution is in order. The depth of many of St. Augustine's responses is such that to read too many of them in one sitting can cause a degree of spiritual indigestion. The Greek adage *much not many* is the counsel to follow for best results. Certainly, this speaks of Augustine's brilliance, but even more so, it reflects God's splendor.

The contents of this book are fruit of St. Augustine's regular rendezvous with his divine Beloved in his "hermitage within."[3] For it was there that he discovered the One who ultimately answers all our queries and satisfies all our longings.

It is my hope that you will find in Augustine the answers to his questions on prayer. More important, my prayer is that Augustine helps the reader to enter his own hermitage within and there, amid burning desire, discover the "Beauty of ancient days yet ever new."[4]

St. Augustine Answers
101 Questions on Prayer

Chapter 1

The Western World's Most Influential Thinker

Who is this man who has influenced the Western world more than any other writer?

Augustine Aurelius (354-430) was born in North Africa, a part of the Roman Empire, at a time when the empire had been Christian for only a few decades. His mother, Monica, was pious but somewhat passive in her Christian conviction during Augustine's childhood, and he was raised with little or no faith.

He sought the truth and an income in its pursuit, which brought him to Italy, where the real action lay for a young scholar. His teaching career gave way to that of rhetorician (a sort of speech writer at the Imperial Court), since, it turned out, he could command language more easily than mischievous students. He wandered in and out of the shadows until he discovered the fullness of truth and asked to be baptized into the Church.

He was ordained priest and immediately thereafter ordained bishop, a task he undertook with misgivings but much selfless zeal. He was shepherd to the Northern African diocese of Hippo for forty years, and died to the echoes of Vandal hordes ravaging the city he had served with paternal love.

So much for the man. Now the mind.

The world has not seen another like his. We Westerners are all under his influence in some way. Perhaps we have not considered the genesis of many of the concepts that make up our worldview, but in many cases, they are Augustine's progeny. Indeed, thinking like a Westerner means thinking like Augustine. Nonetheless, his intellectual reach is not confined to Christian philosophy and theology. Even the twentieth-century existentialists were under his spell when they appropriated his notion of "alienation" and called it their own.

Amongst other Augustinian concepts that pervade our culture are:

- Understanding God as a deep inner presence.

- Grace as an interior help.

- Free will as a faculty uninhibited by external coercion as an integral feature of our souls.

- The claim that words and gestures are signs that express our souls and personalities.

- The notion of sin as a wandering far from happiness into a dark region where we lose what we love most. Rather than seeing sin superficially as a matter of rule-breaking, he thinks of it as *relationship*-breaking. For him, sin's wages are paid in loneliness, grief, and misery.

- The view that each one of us is an "I" in search of a relationship with God, the only "You" who can satiate the soul.

That last notion, the soul as an infinite void with unlimited capacity because made for union with God, is perhaps Augustine's most renowned. Its characteristic quality is a yearning for satisfaction that nothing finite can gratify. Having insufficient resources of its own on which to draw and left to itself, the soul is condemned to its own native nothingness. It is compelled to search for a compatible "Other," lest it be absorbed by this hollow restlessness. God lets himself be found. And when he is found, what was once a vacuum of loneliness is transformed into a place of refuge, a veritable "hermitage within," where our heart can rest and enjoy converse with the Lord.

At this point it should be clear that God is the key to understanding the majority of Augustine's thought. In that light, we make it to port only if we succeed in loving God. Our happiness would never cease if we could just love God more than ourselves.

In great part, Augustine's influence had time and place on its side. As his dates suggest, he lived in what is known as Late Antiquity, on the threshold of the Middle Ages; an age which would construct its intellectual traditions largely on the foundation of his ideas. He carried out his ecclesiastical mission in the Roman Empire as a Roman citizen, in spite of being raised in North Africa. For intellectual sustenance, his youth was filled with the classics of Roman literature, Virgil and Cicero primarily. And his sojourn in Italy provided him with important contacts in the world of literature, ideas, and the life of the Church, all of which helped to shape his work as well as give it a broader scope and audience. Thus equipped with the best of nature and grace, Augustine stands on the shoulders of those two Latin giants from his younger days.

More than just a prolific writer, Augustine is also a founder of a school of normative Christian thought. This places him amongst those privileged men who are known as the Church Fathers — gifted and influential writers who helped to interpret Sacred Scripture, unfolding its doctrines and founding the discipline of theological reflection. And from amongst them, he is undoubtedly one of the greatest.

This is the man who wants to answer our questions about prayer. Few are as up to the task as Augustine: Doctor and Father of the Church, bishop and founder of a monastic order, saint and mystic.

Chapter 2

The Nature of Prayer

1. What is prayer?

Although "the nature of prayer is so complex,"[5] prayer can be compared to "the breath of the soul. It is like incense, which rises to the holy altar. There is no perfume more fragrant.[6] This life is for praying,[7] (while) in heaven there will be no praying, only praising.[8] Prayer is a spiritual reality, made more pleasing inasmuch as it is done according to its nature.[9] In prayer we turn to God alone,[10] because in that state we are all beggars before God;[11] and in our indigence, we can only plead.[12]

2. What happens in prayer?

More than presenting God with a wish list of what we want from him, prayer is God's means to prepare our souls for what he wants to give us. "The Lord our God wants us to petition him, not in order to inform him . . . but in order that by our prayer we might exercise that desire by which we are prepared to receive what he wants to bestow upon us. His gifts are magnificent, but we are small, and our ability to receive is constrained. Therefore, he said, *be open yourselves. Do not be yoked with unbelievers* (2 Cor. 6:12, 14). For in proportion to our simplicity of faith, firmness of hope, and ardor of desire, we will be able to be more open to receive what is immensely great, which *neither eye has seen, nor ear has heard;* and *what has not entered into the heart of man*, for the heart of man must ascend to it."[13] Prayer in this life is preparation for communion with God in eternal life.

Chapter 3

Getting Started

3. What do I need to begin to pray?

To pray, one needs *desire*. "Your desire is itself your prayer. And if your desire is continuous, then your prayer is continuous as well."[14]

4. What else will help me along the way in the life of prayer?

"Fasting and abstinence from satisfying sensual pleasure in such a way that health is not threatened, along with almsgiving are especially helpful to prayer, in order to say truly, "*When in trouble I sought the Lord, all night long I stretch out my hands*" (Ps. 77: 2). How can God, intangible Spirit, be touched by hands by any other way than by good works?"[15]

5. So prayer is more than words?

"*With my voice I have cried to the Lord*. It did not suffice to say 'with voice,' and it was not unintentional that the word 'my' was added. Many cry out to the Lord, not with their own voice, but with their corporeal voice alone. Let the 'inner man' in whom *Christ dwells by faith* (Eph. 3:17), cry out to the Lord, not with the noise of lips alone, but with the affection of the heart. God does not hear as men hear. Unless you cry out with a voice from the depths of your lungs and with your tongue, men will not hear you. Unless you cry out to the Lord with your thought, the Lord does not hear you. Your thought is your cry. *With my voice I have prayed to the Lord*. What he meant by 'I have cried out to the Lord' is explained when he says, 'I have prayed unto the Lord' . . . First, he speaks of his crying, then he explained what it was, as if an explanation were demanded of him: with what kind of cry have you cried out to the Lord? He responds, I have prayed unto the Lord. My cry is not reviling, murmuring, nor blaspheming, but simply my prayer."[16]

6. Where is all of this leading?

"We would keep vigil, yet we fall asleep. We want to fast, and we hunger and thirst. We want to stand and we tire ourselves out and wish to sit, yet if we do this for long, we weary. No matter what we provide for our refection, we find defection . . . What, then, is this peace men have who are confronted with so many difficulties, trials, desires, wants, and weariness? . . . What will be his peace? *For that which is corruptible must clothe itself with incorruptibility, and that which is mortal must clothe itself with immortality* (1 Cor. 15:53) . . . For where mortality is still to be found, how can there be full peace there? It is from death that such weariness comes, just as we find it in all our means of refreshment . . . When death is swallowed up in victory, these things shall be no longer . . . There shall be peace made pure in the sons of God, all loving one another, seeing one another full of God, since *God shall be all in all* (1 Cor. 15:28). We shall have God as our common object of vision, as our common possession, our common peace. For whatever he gives us now, he shall be to us in place of his present gifts. He shall be our full and perfect peace . . . Our joy, our peace, our rest, the end of our troubles, is none but God."[17]

7. What if I don't feel drawn to prayer?

"No man comes unless he is drawn. There are those he draws, and there are those he does not draw. Do not even consider why he draws one and why he does not draw another, if you do not want to err. Simply accept it and then understand. Are you not drawn? Pray, then, that you might be drawn to him."[18] It is urgent to overcome sentimentalism in our relationship with God. He is far too worthy and our soul too precious to attempt to tread the waters of this life alone and without God's help, or simply with his help when we feel like it.

"There is no sea so deep as the thoughts of God, who makes evil men to flourish and the good to suffer — nothing so profound, nothing so deep. And it is upon that deep, in that profundity that every unbelieving soul is wrecked. Do you want to cross over the deep? Then do not move away from the wood of Christ's Cross. You shall not sink; just hold tight to Christ."[19]

Chapter 4

Prayer and the Presence of God

8. What should I look for when I go into myself?

Augustine counsels us to seek a light both within us and beyond us.

Where God is there is peace. With this in mind, Augustine counsels seeking such peace, which he beautifully calls "the Sabbath of the heart. For it listens to God, who promises great things, and if it labors in the present, it expands in hope of the future, where the clouds of sadness are brightened; as the apostle says, *rejoice in hope* (Rom. 12:12). And that very joy in the tranquility of our hope is our Sabbath."[20]

More than merely counsel it, he leads the way:

"Thus being admonished to return to myself, I did enter into my interior self, led on by you. Indeed, I could do so, because you became my helper. And I entered. With the eye of my soul (such as it was) I saw above the very eye of my soul, beyond my mind, Light unchangeable. Not that mundane light, which all things corporal can see, but one of the same kind yet stronger still, almost as though its splendor could have been yet stronger, enough to fill all things with its greatness. Such was not like that light, but different, indeed, quite different from all such as those. Nor was it above my mind as oil is above water. Neither was it as heaven is above earth. It was, nonetheless, above because it created me. And I, having been made by it, stand below it."[21]

9. What do I need to discover this Light?

Love. "He who knows the truth, knows what that light is; and he who knows it, knows eternity. Love knows it. O Truth eternal and true love and beloved eternity, you are my God, for you I long night and day. When I first knew you, you lifted me up in order to see, yet I was not yet capable. You repelled the infirmity of my vision, forcefully streaming forth beams of your light upon me that I trembled with love and awe. I sensed that I was far removed from you, away in the region of unlikeness. And I seemed to hear a voice from on high: 'I am the food for grown men. Grow and you shall feed on me. But you shall not transform me, as you do with your food, but you will be transformed into me.' "[22]

10. So our prayer is a search for a transcendent and yet immanent God?

God is he who is most remote and most present;[23] most high yet closest;[24] more intimate than my most intimate part and higher than the highest part of me;[25] internal and external;[26] "Without interruption or occupying space, with his immutable and exalted power, God is the most interior of all things, because all things exist in him. Further, he is the most external thing, because he is above them all. Thus . . . with his immutable eternity he is the oldest of all things and the first of all things; he is the newest, because he comes after them all."[27]

"Too late have I loved you, O Beauty of ancient days yet ever new. Too late have I loved you. For while you were within, I was away, yet all the while I sought you. Deformed, I cast myself among those beautiful forms you had made. You were with me, but I was not with you. Such things kept me far from you, which, unless they were in you, did not exist at all."[28]

11. If God is transcendent and immanent, why are we enjoined to go *into our private room and, with the door shut, pray to our Father who is in a secret place?* (cf. Matt. 6:6)

"*With full voice I cry to the Lord; with full voice I beseech the Lord* (Ps. 142:2). What does it mean to pour out supplications before him? What is 'before him'? (What is) in his sight. But what is 'in His sight'? Wherever he can see. But where does he not see? Do we not say, 'wherever he can see' as if there were somewhere where he could not see? . . . He sees where man does not see. No man sees your thoughts, but God does. So pour out your prayer where God alone sees, he who repays all. For the Lord Jesus Christ enjoined you to pray in private. But if you know what 'your private room' is and clean it, then pray to God there. *And when you pray, go into your private room and, when you have shut your door, pray to your Father who is in that secret place, and your Father who sees all that is done in secret will reward you.* If men are to reward you, pour out your prayer before men. If God is to reward you, pour out your prayer before him; and close the door, lest the tempter enter."[29]

12. But what does it mean to "shut the door"?

St. Augustine makes of the "door" the human heart, where man is alone with God. But to be alone with God in the sanctuary of the human heart, certain preparatory steps must be taken to ensure an authentic encounter with him. "Cast out of your heart all sordid desires . . . greed . . . superstitions, blasphemies, and evil thoughts. Throw away your resentment — not only those you harbor toward your friends but those for your enemy, too. Take away all those things, then enter into your heart, and there you will find joy. And when you have thus rejoiced, the very purity of your heart will delight you and impel you to pray . . . Enter, purify everything, lift your eyes to the Lord, and he will hear you."[30] There, the man of prayer "goes into himself and turns toward the Father, finding in him the safest refuge . . . He is freed of himself in order to be united to God."[31]

Augustine speaks of his own experience of entering and shutting in order to be alone with God: "You were before me, yet I had distanced myself from myself and could not find myself — much less could I find you."[32] "Admonished by those writings to turn inward I entered into my inward self under your guidance. I was able to because you had become my Helper. I did enter and with eye of my soul — as murky as it was — and saw above the eye of my soul, above my mind, the Unchangeable Light."[33]

13. Does this mean that beyond going into a private room, we *are* that private room? In other words, we are the temples where God is to be found?

"It is clear to us, although we went outward, we were meant to go inward. If only I could find that you said it was to be upon some high and lonely mountain! Since God is on high, I think that he hears me from the heights. Just because you are on a mountain, do you think yourself to be closer to God? Or that he hears you better because you call him from the closest place . . . ? Do you seek a mountain? Descend that he may come closer to you. Or do you choose to ascend? Go up, but not by seeking a mountain. *The heights*, it is said, *are in his heart, in the valley of weeping*. The valley is humility. Therefore, carry out everything interiorly. Even though you seek some high place, a holy place, make of yourself an earthly temple of God. *For the temple of God is holy, and you are that temple*. Do you want to pray in a temple? Pray within yourself. Be first a temple of God, because he hears him who prays in his temple."[34]

Chapter 5

Prayer and Desire: Longing for God

14. I sense a longing for something that I cannot explain — actually, it's more like a void that can't be filled. Is this normal?

Very normal.

This is a natural phenomenon, born of your rapport with your Creator. Augustine calls this earthly life, "the time we have for prayer, while in our eternal home, we will only have time to praise God."[35] "You were made to be a contemplative because praying "is a spiritual thing and is all the more enjoyable the more fully it is done according to our nature."[36] "Because praying and hoping are constant realities of human existence,"[37] "they are the only hopes we have among the many ills of this world."[38]

Our natural desire for God presents us with the dilemma of having to change ourselves, and in doing so we alter our relationship with God. Through prayer we "turn to him alone"[39] "in order to reach him."[40]

15. Isn't it expecting too much to think that anything can truly fill us in this life?

Prayer, the exercise of your relationship with God, is what fills that void, and it is the only natural filler. All other substitute loves will let you down. Praying is as natural as breathing, because, "prayer is the breath of the soul."[41] More than a void, St. Augustine calls it an "abyss." "For what is more profound than an abyss? We see what men do by the movement of their bodies, the words they say; but who can penetrate another's thoughts, who can see into the heart? What is going on inside someone else, what he is inwardly capable of, what he does in his interior, or what his intentions are . . . who can comprehend that? Do not believe that there is a man so profound who can fathom the depths of his own interior."[42] "There let us dwell in hope, since we do not yet dwell in reality . . . And that which was our hope will become our reality, it will be our repose. We shall be visible to ourselves."[43]

Our interior thirsts for God, sometimes without our intellect knowing exactly what it is searching for.

"You are great, O Lord, and greatly to be praised; great is your power, and of your wisdom there is no end. And man, as a part of your creation, desires to praise you, man, who carries within himself his own mortality, that witness of his sin and still more, the witness that you *resist the proud*. Yet man, but a particle of your creation, desires to praise you. You move us to delight in praising you; for you have made us for yourself, and our hearts are restless till they find rest in you."[44]

Chapter 6

Seeking God in Prayer

16. Where should I look for God?

Augustine points us to our interior, to our "hermitage within where no man can see,"[45] where we are alone with God.

"It is difficult to find Christ in a crowd. Your mind needs a certain solitude, for it is only by this type of contemplative solitude that God is seen. A crowd has noise, yet this seeing requires secrecy . . . Do not seek Christ in a crowd: He is not like one from among the crowd, for he excels every crowd."[46]

"There is One who hears your prayer, therefore, do not hesitate to pray; for he who hears dwells within. You needn't turn your eyes toward the mountain, nor raise your face toward the stars or the sun or the moon. Nor must you believe yourself to be heard [better] because you pray near the sea. Rather, despise those prayers.

"But purify the chamber of your heart. Regardless of where you are, there pray, for he who dwells within — in that secret place which the psalmist calls the bosom — hears you . . . Our Lord God is here, the Word of God, the Word made flesh, the Son of the Father, the Son of God, the Son of Man; the lofty One who makes us, the humble one who makes us anew, walking among men, bearing the human, concealing the divine."[47]

17. But isn't this "going into ourselves" thing narcissistic?

More than introversion, prayer is transcendence of oneself. St. Augustine says this beautifully in the following text:

"Do not wander outside of yourself, but return into yourself, for within the interior man dwells the truth. And when you have discovered that you, too, are mutable, transcend yourself. You transcend a reasoning soul. Therefore, gravitate toward that place where your reason is illuminated."[48] "Christ dwells in the interior man."[49]

Augustine goes on to say, "You were in front of me; but I had gone far away from myself, yet did not find myself — much less did I find you."[50] God, "the eternal internal,"[51] who is "the most secret and most present"[52] induces man to seek after him. The sense of God's absence is where he starts. Man seeks him because he is absent, but knows him and finds him because he is present. "Where were you then for me, and how far away? And I was a wanderer far away from you . . . But you were more internal than what was intimate in me, and higher than what was highest in me."[53] "You were with me, and I was not with you."[54]

In other words, St. Augustine suggests the polar opposite of narcissism. Prayer is entrance into a relationship that elevates it to "where (divine) light illumines the soul."[55] The light is Christ, for "Christ dwells in the interior man."[56] Christ elevates the soul of the person in whom he dwells, so as to make communion and dialog possible. Rather than introverted narcissism, Christ liberates us through grace and prayer, all made possible by his loving presence in our souls.

18. In other words, prayer is not an extra, but is a part of the fulfillment of our nature?

Exactly. This was Augustine's own experience. His famous line, "You have made us for yourself, and our hearts are restless until they rest in you,"[57] sums it up. We can fully understand ourselves only in the context of our relationship with God. Man's capacity to have a relationship with God in this life through prayer points to man's ultimate destiny — to enjoy God through the direct vision of him in heaven. Man is "is the image of the one whom he is capable of enjoying, and whose partner he can become."[58] In other words, man "has been created in such an excellent state that even although it is itself mutable, it reaches happiness by cleaving to the unchangeable good; that is, to God. Nor can it satisfy its need unless it is totally happy; and only God suffices to satisfy it."[59]

This also helps to respond to the question of man's interiority as an opportunity to encounter God, and not an exercise in spiritual narcissism. Thus Augustine counsels, "Go back into yourself; the truth dwells in the inner man; and if you discover that your nature is mutable, transcend yourself also."[60]

19. Does that mean my inclination to pray is part of my nature? That I've come prepackaged for an encounter with God?

Yes. That's how God woos the soul. He has made you for himself, *capax Dei*,[61] or capable of entering into a relationship with him. If he has made you capable of that relationship, it is because he wants to have an intimate relationship with you. "He, therefore, who makes it possible for even such as the rich to enter the kingdom of heaven, has instilled in you such pious concern to the point that you deem it necessary to ask my advice on how you should pray. While on earth, he brought rich Zacchaeus into the kingdom of heaven. And being glorified in his resurrection and ascension, he brought many rich men to hold this present world in disdain, and thus truly enriching them by granting them the Holy Spirit and thereby extinguishing all longing for wealth. Otherwise, how could you have such desire for prayer if your hope were not placed in him? And how could you trust in Him if your trust were placed in those unstable riches, all the while ignoring the apostle's saving counsel: *Tell the rich in the present age not to be proud and not to rely on so uncertain a thing as wealth but rather on God, who richly provides us with all things for our enjoyment. Tell them to do good, to be rich in good works, to be generous, ready to share, thus accumulating as treasure a good foundation for the future, so as to win the life that is true life.* (1 Tim. 6:17-19)."[62]

Chapter 7

Finding God in Prayer

20. If God wants me to find him, why does he play hide-and-seek with me?

If man is an enigma unto himself, we should not be surprised that God proves to be even more sublime. "Every man is a stranger in this life, in which you see that we have an unseen heart wrapped with flesh . . . In this earthly life's sojourn each one bears his own heart, and every heart is hidden to every other heart."[63] The unfathomed depths of our interior are the place where this search for God begins. But simply beginning the search is, to a certain extent, already to have begun to bridge the gap between God and ourselves. It enables us to enter into the mind of God, and from that point of vantage to contemplate God's work and the mysteries of faith. To arrive at this view of reality, the search has to begin, which entails shedding the skin of human wisdom and prudence. These steps in God's direction, the search for him, are what occasion the Holy Spirit's illumination, for, "Similarly, no one knows what pertains to God except the Spirit of God. *We have not received the spirit of the world but the Spirit that is from God, so that we may understand the things freely given us by God. And we speak about them not with words taught by human wisdom, but with words taught by the Spirit, describing spiritual realities in spiritual terms. Now the natural person does not accept what pertains to the Spirit of God, for to him it is foolishness, and he cannot understand it, because it is judged spiritually. The spiritual person, however, can judge everything but is not subject to judgment by anyone. For "who has known the mind of the Lord, so as to counsel him?" But we have the mind of Christ* (1 Cor. 2:11-16). The search for God, then, has the function of transforming our minds, which, in turn, transforms our hearts."[64]

21. Is God to be sought even after we have found him?

"Such is the way with incomprehensible things — they must be investigated so that no one believe he has found a mere nothing, when in fact he has been able to find how incomprehensible that is which he was seeking . . . And making progress in the search itself, he becomes ever better while seeking so great a good . . . For it is both sought in order that in finding it, it may be more sweetly enjoyed, and found that it be all the more zealously sought. The words of Wisdom in the book of Ecclesiasticus may be understood thus: *they who eat me will hunger for more, they who drink me will thirst for more* (Ecclus. 24:29). For they eat and drink because they find; and yet their search continues, as do their hunger and thirst. Faith seeks, understanding finds; thus the prophet says, *Unless you believe, you shall not understand* (Isa. 7:9). And yet, again, understanding still seeks him whom it finds; for *Yahweh is looking down from heaven at the sons of men*, as it is sung in the holy Psalm, *to see if any are wise, if a single one is seeking God* (Ps. 14:2). And man, therefore, needs understanding that he might seek after God."[65]

Chapter 8

Prayer and Conversion

22. What is the relationship between prayer and conversion?

Before conversion: man is without God. Augustine says such a man is lost in the deep, "for our depths is this mortal life. Whoever knows himself to be in the depths cries out with groans and sighs until he is delivered from the depths, and comes to him whose seat is above all . . . until his own image, that image which is man, who in these depths has been thrown about by constant waves and worn away by them, is freed by God. And unless he is made anew and aright by God, who impressed (that image) on him when he formed man, he will remain in the depths. Although man is equal to his own fall, he is not equal to the task of his own rising. Unless he is freed, he remains in the depths. But once he cries out from the depths, he rises because his very cry will not suffer him to be at the bottom for long."[66]

Context of the conversion. In that condition of self-knowledge and recognition of his own sinfulness and helplessness when left to himself, and "in order that men might not live even worse off through despair, God promised a safe harbor of forgiveness. Further, that they might not live the worse from hope of pardon, God made man's date with death uncertain — thus establishing both most providentially, as a refuge for his return and a terror to his vacillation."[67]

Three conversions through trial. Each trial is overcome by prayer — "crying out to the Lord." Once man "is roused to seek the grace of God, and to become anxious, and to awaken from his slumber — is it not God's hand that arouses him? Nonetheless, he does not know that it was God who awakened him; yet more and more he begins to belong to God now that he has come to know and believe the Truth. But before that can occur, he must grieve over his error. Because, finding himself in error, he longs for the Truth, knocking where he may, trying out what he can, sensing a hungering for the Truth. *This first trial is one of wandering and hunger.* Once he has had enough of this trial and is brought to call out to God, he takes to the way of faith, that path whose journey will bring him to the city of Peace. For it is Christ who leads him, Christ who said, *I am the Way* (John 14:6).

"When he has taken to the path, he grows weary, for he knows how he should live, but at times, having attributed too much to himself, presumptuous of his strength, he attempts to fight against his sins, but in his pride it just gets worse. He is bound by desire, whose bonds impede his walking on the way. He is a prisoner of vice . . . unable to escape. He knows how he ought to live . . . unlike before, but how to accomplish this is beyond him. He is in shackles and cries to the Lord. *The second trial is that of how to do good, whereas the first was that of wandering and hunger.* In his crying to the Lord, he is heard and the Lord breaks his chains of difficulty, and establishes him in acting righteously. What had previously been difficult is now made easy for him. To abstain from every sort of sin has not become easy. God could have granted this without difficulties, but if there were no difficulties, we would not appreciate the Giver of this good gift. For if man at first did not feel the weight of desire's chains whenever he wished, and his soul were not wounded by the weight of its chains, he would think to attribute what he was now able to do to his own strength, never confessing the mercies of the Lord.

"After those two trials, man is overcome by a third trial . . . Having been freed from every sort of sin with the help of the Holy Spirit, so that wishing not to be an adulterer, he is not; wishing not to be a thief, he is not, etc., such a man is met with a third trial. *This trial is a sort of lethargy one feels at the length of his life, finding no enjoyment in prayer or reading.* Contrary to the first trial, which was a hungering, this trial is distaste for food. What is the origin of this trial but a certain apathy of spirit? Adultery no longer attracts you, but neither does the word of God delight you. Now, after the danger of ignorance and concupiscence, from which you rejoice at having escaped, be on guard that this inertia and disgust do not overtake you. This is no small trial either. Cry out to the Lord that he may free you of these circumstances, and once freed from this trial, confess his mercies to him."[68]

Counsels for the converted. To have gone through conversion, it is clear that things cannot remain the same. But the Christian on the way of faith encounters many who do not take his same path, for he is still in the world he left. "[F]or living among things human, we cannot withdraw from things human. We must live among evil men with forbearance, because when we used to be evil men, the good men lived with forbearance among us. If we do not forget what we have been, we will not despair of those who are now what we once were."[69]

As prayer accompanied the three conversions, it should also take the form of gratitude for God's mercy as well as intercession for those lagging behind on the way or who have not taken to it yet.

Chapter 9

Prayer and Grace

23. What is more important: prayer or grace?

The necessity of prayer is bound essentially to the necessity of grace, since, "God has desired that in spiritual combat we might fight rather with prayers than with our own strength."[70] For Augustine, the need of prayer and the need of grace are bound up together. "God does not command the impossible, but when he commands, he orders you to do what you can and to ask for what you cannot do on your own in order that he help you to do what you cannot accomplish on your own . . . [T]he very fact that we believe with the firmest faith that the just and good God could not command the impossible makes us see what we ought to do in easy situations and what we ought to do in difficult ones. As a result, all situations become easy for charity that grace has inspired in our hearts."[71]

With that in mind, it is clear that we do not fight alone. Further, we do not simply have God on our side: living in a state of grace, we have God within us. "It is said that the Holy Spirit dwells in those persons in virtue of his secret action within their souls, in such a way that they become his temple, which he brings to perfection in those who progress and are persevering in progress . . . In those in whom he dwells, the Holy Spirit begins the construction of his own dwelling place, which he finishes, not in this life, but in the one after this, *when death will be absorbed by victory*, and it will be said: *Death is swallowed up in victory. Where, O death, is your victory? Where, O death, is your sting?* (1 Cor. 15:55)."[72]

To have the Blessed Trinity within us is an ineffable gift. To have God dwelling within means to have heaven, God's glory, already on this earth, but in an invisible way. This means a certain paradigm shift in the way heaven is frequently understood. Heaven is not what comes *after* this life. In grace heaven already accompanies us — from the inside. This means that eternity is in the here and now. "Join your heart to the eternity of God, and with him you will be eternal . . . Join yourself to the eternity of God, and together with him wait for those things which are beneath you. Because when you heart cleaves to God, all mortal things are beneath you."[73]

"God gives help so that the command becomes possible,"[74] since "he does not abandon us unless we abandon him first. And what is abandonment of God — 'death's sting' — if not sin itself?"[75]

To persevere in grace requires our active cooperation. "It is certain that God has prepared some gifts even for those who do not pray, such as the beginning of faith; but other gifts only for those who pray, such as final perseverance."[76] Thus prayer is the means of obtaining grace, but is also the effect of grace.

24. Do we really have to pray for God's grace? Can't we make it on our own?

Augustine's nemesis was Pelagius, an English monk who believed that man was capable of saving himself. To those who thought they could go it alone, without necessary recourse to God's grace, Augustine had the following to say: "The Pelagians think themselves possessors of a great truth when they say that

God would not give an order if he knew we could not possibly fulfill it. But who does not know that? Rather, it is precisely because of this that God orders us to do things that we cannot do so that we understand what we should ask for from him. Faith is that which — with prayer — obtains what the law commands."[77] "They [the Pelagians] attribute much power to the will but at the cost of prayer, of Christian piety."[78]

Augustine wanted to protect the role of grace in the order of salvation, while at the same time maintaining man's free will. Prayer plays an all-important role in the paradigm of grace/free will/salvation. Only grace can save us, but we need freely to ask for it in order to receive it — hence, our prayer of petition. "God does not command the impossible, but orders you to do what you can, and to ask for what you cannot do, and he helps you to do it all."[79] Notice how Augustine's theology of grace protects human freedom ("do what you can"), which requires divine assistance ("God helps you to do it all"), but only if we ask God through prayer ("ask for what you cannot do").

Clearly, our weakness expressed in our prayer of petition makes a perfect match for God's strength, manifest in his grace. Thus, St. Augustine can pray, "Give to me what you command of me, and demand of me whatever you want."[80]

"When the Lord tells us *convert to me and I will convert to you*, what else is he saying than: 'do what I command you'? And when we say to the Lord: 'turn to us, Lord, and we will turn to you,' what else are we saying than: 'give us what we need to accomplish what you command'?"[81]; "(for) the law was therefore given, in order that grace might be sought [through prayer]; grace was given, in order that the law might be fulfilled."[82]

At the end of the day, both prayer and grace are necessary for salvation. Prayer is born of grace yet effects it, too. The grace of prayer brings us still more grace and the strength we need to fulfill the will of God.

"We fight more with our prayer than we do with our efforts, because these efforts, although necessary, are submitted and ordered by him who prays."[83] "[So] fight with prayer to overcome the world."[84]

25. St. Augustine speaks of obtaining grace for oneself through prayer. Can we obtain grace for *others* through prayer? Is there a social element to prayer?

Augustine speaks amply about our ability to win grace for others, but also about the Christian duty to do so. He sees this responsibility founded primarily on human relationships:

• *Friends pray for each other:* "Many more thanks still shall be yours, if you not only claim an interest in my prayers, but also do not cease praying for me. For intercession on behalf of a brother is more pleasing to God when offered as an oblation of love."[85]

• *Augustine's mother's prayer effected not only his conversion, but his father's as well.* "Finally, her own husband, toward the end of his earthly life, was won over for you . . . Whoever knew her, glorified, honored and loved you in her, for it was through her witness and the fruit of her holy conversation, that they all perceived your presence in her heart. Indeed, she had been the wife of one man, was faithful to her parents, guided her household in a holy way, was renowned for good works, raised her children after having suffered the travail of each one's birth, and saw them serve you."[86]

• *Augustine prayed for all humanity including the Church's persecutors.* "We pray for all the human race, for the entire world, for all people . . . We do so that they correct themselves and become pure of heart, turning to God and his rectitude, and thus adhere to him."[87]

• *For conversions:* every faithful within the Church prays for those who are outside of her. But what does he ask? "Lord, in this time which is under the reign of grace, save sinners, save infidels, save the sterile."[88]

• *For each other's conversion and forgiveness.*[89]

• *For those who do not seem predestined to salvation:* "Let us pray for those not yet called, that they may be called. It could happen that they are predestined in the following way: that their salvation is dependent upon our prayer in such a way that through it they receive the grace to choose to be among the elect."[90]

• *For those suffering injustices:* in this case, Augustine is speaking about three sisters who have been kidnaped. "Pray to God for them, and beg him to enable them to say what holy Azariah said, as we have mentioned, who poured out his prayer and witness before God."[91]

• *Pastors and faithful should pray for each other.*[92]

Chapter 10

Prayer and Salvation

26. What about non-believers?

St. Augustine speaks primarily about praying for all those people who are parts of our lives. But he does not limit prayer's range of action to them. He also counsels prayer for the enemies of the faith and those who are outside the Church.

"And if any of you are not yet called, we should pray for them that they indeed be called. It might be that they are so predestined to be included in our prayers and thereby receive the grace by which they are counted amongst the elect." For God, who has fulfilled all that he predestines, wants us to pray for the enemies of the faith, too, so that we would in turn see that it is he who gives to the unbelievers, too, the gift of faith. And it is he who makes men who formerly were unwilling, to become men who do will it."[93]

27. How does our prayer play a part in predestination?

The concept of predestination ruffles all sorts of feathers. Augustine treats the theme differently according to the audience he is addressing. In a simple but convincing passage, he holds that our prayer is part of God's plan of salvation for others. In other words, God wants to incorporate our prayer into his saving plan. The only way to know whether our prayer cooperates in the salvation of others is to pray and trust.

"God has so desired it that we ask him that we not be led into temptation . . . He might have given us this even if we had never prayed for it, but it is precisely by our prayer that he wants to remind us from whom we receive such benefits. For from whom do we receive but from him who it is fitting to ask? Therefore, the Church should not seek onerous disputations, but tend to its daily prayers. She prays that the incredulous might believe; hence, God converts them to the faith. She prays that believers persevere; hence, God grants them final perseverance. God foreknew that he would do all of this. And this is the predestination of the saints, *whom he has chosen in him, before the foundation of the world, to be holy and without blemish before him. In love he destined us for adoption to himself through Jesus Christ, in accord with the favor of his will, for the praise of the glory of his grace that he granted us in the beloved.*

In him we have redemption by his blood, the forgiveness of transgressions, in accord with the riches of his grace that he lavished upon us. In all wisdom and insight, he has made known to us the mystery of his will in accord with his favor that he set forth in him as a plan for the fullness of times, to sum up all things in Christ, in heaven and on earth. In him we were also chosen, destined in accord with the purpose of the one who accomplishes all things according to the intention of his will (Eph. 1:4-11). Against a trumpet of truth as clear as that, what man of sober and vigilant faith could accept dispute?"[94]

28. Does this mean that Augustine counts himself among "the elect," and therefore not in need of prayer?

Nothing could be farther from the truth. Given prayer's singular role in the order of salvation, St. Augustine humbly entrusts himself to his readers' prayers.

"When you find me in these books, pray that I might not fail, but reach perfection. Pray, my son, pray. I feel what I say and understand what I ask. Do not let it seem something unbecoming or too elevated for you. You would cheat me of great help if you were not to do so. But not only you, but anyone who by your witness should come to love me, let him pray for me, too. Read Sacred Scriptures, and you will discover that the Apostles, shepherds of Christ's flock, asked it of their hearers. And since you ask it of me, I will most certainly do so for you to the best of my ability. He who sees this is the Hearer of all prayer, and it was he who saw that I had already prayed for you even before you asked it of me. We have been placed over you, for you are of God's flock. Take note that our dangers are graver than yours — so pray for us; this is most becoming of us and you, that, in this way, we might be able to render good accounts of you to the Chief Shepherd and Head over us all. Thus we might escape the tribulations and the seductions of this world, which are more dangerous, except when the peace of this world has the effect for which the apostle enjoins us to pray, *that we may lead a quiet and peaceful life in all godliness and honesty* . . . Ask, then, for us what we ask for you, that we might lead a quiet and peaceful life in all godliness and honesty. Let's ask this for each other wherever you may be or I, for he to whom we belong is ever present."[95]

Chapter 11

Effective Prayer

29. How can I guarantee that God will hear my prayer?

"*Bow down your ear, O Lord, and hear me.* He speaks as a servant: speak, O servant, in the form of your Lord: *Bow down your ear, O Lord.* He does indeed bow down his ear, if you do not lift up your neck; for the Lord draws near to the humble man. But from the exalted man he distances himself, unless he himself has exalted that man for his humility. God then bows down his ear toward us. For he is on high, we below; he is in a high place, we in a lowly yet not yet desolate place.

"*Indeed, only with difficulty does one die for a just person, though perhaps for a good person one might even find courage to die. But God proves his love for us in that while we were still sinners Christ died for us* (Rom. 5:8). It was not because of our merits that the Son of God had gone to his death, but on the contrary, because we had no merits and his mercy was great . . . Unto the humble and the one who confesses to him his need of mercy, God bows down his ear. But not to him who is full of himself, who boasts and lifts himself up, as if he were not needy, as if to say *I thank you, God, that I am not like this publican* (Luke 18:11). For the rich Pharisee bragged of his merits, while the poor publican confessed his sins."[97]

30. It sounds as if humility is a prerequisite for prayer. Are there other virtues that prepare the way for effective prayer?

"Faith, hope, and love, therefore, lead the man of prayer to God. That is, the man who believes, hopes, and desires is guided with regard to what he should ask the Lord by study of the Lord's Prayer."[98]

31. What does sacrifice have to do with prayer?

"Encouraging sacrifice, the apostle says, *I beg you, in a way that is worthy of thinking beings, to offer your bodies as a living sacrifice, holy and pleasing to God* (Rom. 12:1). If the soul uses the body — which is inferior — as an instrument or a servant, thus becoming a sacrifice when used correctly and in reference to God, how much more must the soul, in turn, become a sacrifice when it offers itself to God, so that, aflame with the fire of God's love, it might participate in his beauty and become pleasing to him? For it has lost the old form of earthly desire and has been remolded according to the image of eternal beauty. And to this the apostle adds, *Do not conform yourselves to this age but be transformed by the renewal of your mind, that you may discern what is the will of God, what is good and pleasing and perfect* (Rom. 12:2)."[99]

32. What is the relation between faith and prayer?

"The Holy Gospel instructs us to pray and believe, to put our trust in the Lord, and not in ourselves. What greater motivation to pray could he have given us than the parable of the unjust Judge? . . . [I]f he who hated to be asked heard her prayer, how then must he who counsels us to ask him hear us? Compared to a contrary example, the Lord taught that *men ought to pray without ceasing*, he added, saying, *nonetheless, when the Son of Man comes, do you think that he will find faith on the earth?* If faith lacks, prayer dies. For who prays for that which he does not believe? Thus, the blessed Apostle counseled prayer saying, *whoever calls on the name of the Lord shall be saved.* And to illustrate that faith is the foundation of prayer, he added, *How, then, shall they call on him in whom they have not believed?* So that we might pray, let us believe. And that this faith by which we pray not fail, let us pray. Faith pours out prayer and the pouring out of prayer, in turn, obtains the strengthening of faith."[100]

33. So is faith merely the source of prayer?

For St. Augustine faith is more than prayer's source. It is certainly more than trusting that his prayers are heard. *Faith proves the existence of realities that at present remain unseen* (Heb. 11:1). These are the mysteries of the spiritual life, whether they pertain to the life of the Blessed Trinity or to the economy of its communication to humanity through Christ's Sacred Humanity. Thus, God alone knows the things of God in their fullness: *the depths of God can only be known by the Spirit of God* (1 Cor. 2:11). But he does communicate something of himself to man, and that is precisely the content of Augustine's faith.

God's holiness is his own vision of himself. His love for himself is infinitely perfect and in proportion to his vision of himself. The measure of that vision that he grants us is the measure of our resemblance to him, through which we tend toward him, just as he tends toward himself. This is what is meant by being pulled toward God, and indeed all love for God is holiness. Knowing God's goodness triggers love for God. There is a gravitational pull of the will toward God's goodness, just as there is a gravitational pull of a weight toward the ground. Hence Augustine speaks of God in his famous phrase *amor meus, pondus meum* ("my love, my weight").[101]

Although we are deprived of the vision of God, given our mortal state, we do attain it to a certain extent by faith. Through faith, we contemplate the truth, albeit without the amenities of the light of vision. *[T]his God has revealed to us through the Spirit . . . We have not received the spirit of the world but the Spirit that is from God, so that we may understand the things freely given us by* God (1 Cor. 2:10, 12). This spirit is the spirit of faith, and the gifts are our participation in divine life which requires our cooperation through prayer.

34. Christ says, *Watch and pray, that you not fall into temptation*. What is the relation between prayer and temptation?

"In order for faith not to fail, the Lord said, *watch and pray, lest you fall into temptation* . . . What is to enter into temptation but to fail in faith? Temptation advances as faith lets up. And temptation yields as faith advances . . . The Lord said, *watch and pray, lest you fall into temptation*, whereby we touch faith, lest it weaken and die. In the same place in the Gospel he said, *this night Satan has sifted you like wheat, but I have prayed for you, Peter, that your faith not fail*. He who fights prays, and would not he who is in danger pray?"[102]

35. So there seem to be degrees of faith. Can we say that the degree of faith we have is determined by our degree of prayer?

"When the Lord said, *when the Son of Man comes, do you think he shall find faith on the earth?* he was speaking of perfect faith. Such faith is scarcely found on this earth. See, this church is full, and who among you would be here if he had no faith? But who would not move mountains if his faith were full? Consider the Apostles: they would never have left all they had, trodden this world's hopes underfoot, and followed the Lord if their faith were not great. And yet, if their faith were perfect, they would not have said to the Lord, *increase our faith*. Consider again that man confessing faith — yet behold an imperfect faith — who presented his son to the

Lord to be freed of an evil spirit, and was asked if he believed. He answered saying, *Lord, I believe. Help my unbelief*. 'I believe': there was faith. But, 'help my unbelief': therefore, this was an imperfect faith."[103]

36. What relation does charity have to prayer?

Only he who has charity obtains what he asks in prayer: "We have confidence in God. Therefore, whatever we ask, we shall receive from him, because we keep his commandments. Thus, where God alone sees, not where men can see, but in our hearts, *we have confidence*, then, *toward God. And whatsoever we ask, we shall receive of him*. How? Because we keep his commandments. What are 'his commandments'? Must we ever repeat it? *I give you a new commandment: love one another.* It is charity itself that he speaks of, it is this that he commands. Whoever has brotherly charity — this means before God, where he can see it — and his heart withstands the interrogation of a just examination of conscience, discovering nothing but the true root of charity from which good fruits come, this man has confidence in God and shall indeed receive from him whatever he asks, because he keeps his commandments."[104]

Chapter 12

The Effects of Prayer on the Soul

37. What effects does prayer bring about in the soul?

"Prayer produces a certain conversion of heart toward him who is always ready to give inasmuch as we are in condition to receive. And in this conversion a purification of the interior eye is wrought in such a way that those things in the temporal order which we used to desire are excluded. In this way the inner eye, having become pure, can withstand the pure light — changeless and never setting — which shines divinely. But not only withstanding the light, it dwells in it, too. And not merely remaining in it unbothered, but it lives in it with ineffable joy, in which consists the truly blessed and perfect life."[105]

Clearly, Augustine is speaking of contemplation, the height of all prayer. In just a few words, our author presents us with a theology of prayer on several levels.

- Prayer effects conversion toward God and aversion from earthly desires.

- The soul undergoes purification in order to grow in the virtue of poverty of spirit.

- The soul is made ready to receive God more fully and indeed comes to dwell in him, in a permanent presence of God.

- The contemplative soul is brought to the perfect joy and blessed life for which she was created.

At the end of it all, the greatest effect of prayer is the love and desire it enkindles and preserves. "And his mercy has taken everything into account. *All that bears fruit*, he says, *should remain; that whatever you shall ask of the Father in my name, he will give it to you*. Similarly, let love remain; for he himself is our gain. And this love remains for the moment as loving desire, an enjoyment not yet completely fulfilled."[106]

Chapter 13

Types of Prayer

38. If contemplation is the height of all prayer, why should we use vocal prayer?

"Relishing continual desire joined to the exercise of faith, hope, and charity, we 'pray always.' Nonetheless, at certain stipulated times we employ words in our prayer to God. And it is by signs such as these that we correct ourselves and discover the degree of progress obtained in this desire, in order to burn even more and achieve an increase in strength. According to the proportion of the ardor of our desire before a prayer is uttered, so will be its effectiveness."[107]

Thus Augustine is saying that the effect of vocal prayer on the soul is threefold:

- It acts as a stimulus.
- It is a gauge with which to measure our growth in prayer.
- It is a means of spiritual growth because it increases desire for God.

Elsewhere, St. Augustine prescribes vocal prayer for his monks — both in community at determined hours of the day and in private according to possibilities and the desire to do so.[108]

He even points to his own experience of vocal prayer in common and private:

"God has said to him, *Offer to God the sacrifice of praise* . . . I will arise daily and make my way to church, and I will say a hymn at matins, another at vespers, the third and fourth I say at home, and daily do I offer the sacrifice of praise and offer myself to my God. You do well if you, too, act thus."[109]

Augustine speaks of prayer as ineffable jubilation arising from the abundance of joy, which can neither be silent nor speak. And on the other hand, it is the recourse of the lonely. "I have read your letter in which you complain of your solitude and being forsaken by your friends . . . But what else could I counsel you than that which you assuredly are already doing: commune with your own soul, elevate it to God as far as you can; because in him you possess even us in a firmer bond."[110]

Thus private prayer is also societal. Inseparable from common prayer, it prepares the soul for a more efficacious common prayer — especially liturgical prayer, which the Second Vatican Council calls the "source and summit" of Christian life.[111]

39. How is the liturgy the "source and summit"?

The call to Sunday Mass had a soothing effect on Augustine's sensitive soul. Man, he says, needs to rest. And what better way to rest than to rest in God?

"Now the souls of men, both good and evil ones, love rest, but how they might attain what they love is for the most part unknown to them. And as bodies seek for their weight, so, too, do souls seek exactly the same thing for their love — a resting place . . . Man's soul struggles onward toward what it loves so that it might rest upon reaching it. When the soul finds its delight in God, there she finds true, certain, eternal rest, for which it had vainly sought in other objects. Hence, the counsel found in the Psalms was laid down, *Find your delight in the LORD, who will give you your heart's desire* (Ps. 37:4)."[112]

Holiness, says Augustine, is linked to the Sabbath.

40. Can song really be counted as prayer?

St. Augustine does not only speak of the merits of sung prayer; he also tells of its effect on his own soul: "How much did I weep at your hymns and canticles, so moved was I by the voices of your dulcet-voiced Church. The voices flowed into my ears and truth poured into my heart, spilling over into my devotion and tears, and thus was I blessed."[113] "When the Church's hymns are clearly sung with wavering voice, I recognize the usefulness of this tradition . . ."[114]

"Behold, he practically intones the hymn for you. Do not search for the words as if you could give form to a hymn that would please God. Sing with jubilation.

"What does 'jubilation' mean? To understand without explaining the word that the heart sings . . . Like those who are so overcome with joy in singing that they cannot express the words of the song and let the syllables drop from their lips and give themselves over to the melody of jubilation. Jubilee is a sort of sound which means that the heart wants to give birth to that which cannot be uttered. And who deserves such jubilation if not the ineffable God? And ineffable is that which cannot be said or even touched. What remains if not jubilation in that the heart opens itself to a wordless joy, and the joy increases beyond the limits of the spoken word?"[115]

"Singing is proper to one in love."[116] Certainly, Augustine had experienced human love, but the divine love which invaded his soul took possession of his whole being. Such a state can be somewhat precarious, and he recognized the importance of protecting the heart weakened by Original Sin from other loves. Hence his proscription of all singing amongst his monks, save that which is prescribed in the *Rule*.[117]

Chapter 14

Prayer of Praise

41. What is praise?

Whereas adoration bows the head before God's majesty, praise raises it up to him, seeking his Face. Since God deserves praise and of his greatness there is no end, "do not think that he can be praised enough whose greatness is endless. Should not then your praise be endless since he has no end?"[118] Thus, our life is a continual seeking of God's Face and praising his name.

St. Augustine knew the human heart in all its depth and weakness. He was aware of the temptation to focus on God's gifts more than on the divine Giver. He cautions his hearers about this and offers some concrete advice on how to avoid this vice.

"*Celebrating your acts of power, one age shall praise your doings to another. Oh, the splendor of your glory, your renown! Men will proclaim your fearful power and I shall relate your greatness; they will celebrate your generous kindness and joyfully acclaim your righteousness* — only yours will act thus. See whether this man, upon meditating on your works, has turned his gaze toward the works and away from the Worker. Observe whether or not he has descended from the Maker of all things to the things he has made. For what he has made has been made as a ladder to ascend to him, not descend from him. For if you love these things more than you love him, you shall not possess him. What does it profit you to have an abundance of works if the Worker should leave you? Certainly, you should love those things, but love him more — and love them for his sake.

"Praise of God sets you on your way and should determine what you ought to love and what you should fear; what you should seek, and what you should avoid . . . The time to choose is at hand. The time of recompense is later. So let the wonders of your deeds (which have no end) be told now . . . so let your praise have no end."[119]

Our author goes on to say, "The silence of the heart is the cooling of charity, the cry of praise is charity's fervor."[120] A life founded on divine love has to express itself in praise: "You are great, O Lord, and greatly to be praised; great is your power, and of your wisdom there is no end. And man, as a part of your creation, desires to praise you, man, who carries within himself his own mortality, that witness of his sin and still more, the witness that you *resist the proud*. Yet man, but a particle of your creation, desires to praise you. You move us to delight in praising you; for you have made us for yourself, and our hearts are restless till they find rest in you."[121] St. Augustine adds, "The thirteen books of my *Confessions* praise the just and good God of my merits and evils. Merits, because he has given them to me; evils, because he has freed me of them."[122]

Praise is such a fundamental element of Christian life, Augustine claims, that he feels compelled to use the following words: "the sum total of man's work is this: to praise God."[123] Yet it is not enough to simply praise God if we truly love him, "What will be your occupation if not that of praising him whom you love and making others love him as you do?"[124]

Augustine establishes praise at a primordial level that goes so far as to aptly define our eternal life:

"Toils and wailing shall cease, prayers diminish, but hymns of praise continue. There shall be the dwelling place of the blessed . . . for he will be present for whom we sigh. *We shall be like him and see him as he is* (1 John 3:2). There our task will be to praise God and enjoy his presence. What else could we ask for when he satisfies our every desire, he who has made all things? We shall dwell and be dwelt in; and be subject to him so *that he may be all in all* (1 Cor. 15:28) . . . Let this then be the sole object of our longing when we have reached that passage, dear brothers. Let us prepare ourselves, then, to rejoice in God — to praise him."[125]

He who has come to truly know God and love him as he ought can truly praise God. "We can exult in the Lord if our praise recognizes in him that only he responds to our desires . . . the rule is very brief: he pleases God who is pleased by God. And, beloved, do not think that this has to do with pleasure. See how many of you oppose God because you are not pleased with his works. True enough, when he wants to work against the will of men, because he is Lord, because he knows what he should do, he does not take into account so much our will as our well-being. Those who would rather that their own will were fulfilled before God's, think to please God with their will, rather than correct their will by conforming it to his. Hence, we cannot exult in him except with praise. Nor can we ask of him, except after we have praised him."[126] Praising him more then, we please him more. And pleasing him more, he pleases us more.

Not being pleased with the nature of God's will can have a natural foundation — above all when his will demands sacrifice and suffering from his children. The conformity of human will to divine will in order to truly praise God is seen most clearly in Jesus Christ in Gethsemane. His human nature felt repulsion for what he knew to be the will of the Father. *Your will be done!* (Matt. 26:42) spoken by Christ in his crisis moment makes possible the most pleasing praise.

42. Does this mean we manipulate God through our charming praise?

"He is not praised in the same way as by those theater-lovers who praise charioteers, hunters, actors of every sort, and by their praising, others are invited to praise, and even urged to shout in unison . . . Our God is not so. He should be praised with the will, loved with charity. He should be loved and praised gratuitously. But what does 'gratuitous' mean? It means praising him for his own sake, and not for the sake of something else. For if you were to praise God that he might give you something else, you cease to love God freely. You would cringe if your wife loved you for your money and, in the event poverty ensued, she would consider adultery. Since you want to be loved freely by your spouse, would you love God with something else in view? *I will praise your name, O Lord, for it is a good thing* . . . Why? Because 'it is a good thing.' I can find nothing better than your name."[127]

43. What makes our praise so pleasing to God?

Integrity of life.

"Would you sing a psalm? Then do not sound God's praises with voice alone, but put your works in harmony with your voice. Sing out with your voice if you would be pleasing to the ear, but do not silence your heart, nor let your life fall silent. Singing a psalm, you commit no vice. When you eat and drink, sing a psalm — not by mixing in harmonious sounds pleasing to the ear, but in moderate eating and drinking with frugality and temperance. For the apostle says, *whatever you eat or drink, whatever you do at all, do it for the glory of God* (1 Cor. 10:31) . . . Even when sleep overcomes you, do not allow an evil conscience to awaken you. In this way, the innocence of your sleep praises God.

"*Let your praises be pleasing to our God*. How? By praising him with the goodness of our lives. Take heed of that, and then your praise will be pleasing to him. Elsewhere it says, *Praise is unseemly in a sinner's mouth* (Ecclus. 15:9). If praise in the mouth of a sinner is unseemly, then it cannot be pleasing, for only what is seemly pleases . . . Perhaps praise pleases man when he hears it with elegant and clever sentiments from a sweet-sounding voice. But 'let praise be pleasant to our God,' whose ears hear what comes not from the mouth but from the heart; not the tongue, but the very life of him who praises."[128]

44. Other than God's deserving our praise, does Augustine offer any motivations to praise God?

"*Oh, the splendor of your glory, your renown . . . Men will proclaim your fearful power, and I shall assert your greatness . . .* Consider whether or not this man who meditates on your work, has descended from him who made all things, to the things he has made. Of those things that he has created, this man has made a ladder to God, rather than descend from God. For if you love them more than you love him, you will not have him. And what does it profit you to have an overflow of works if the Worker abandons you? Certainly, you should love them, but love him more. For he does not extend promises without extending threats. If he held out no promise, there would be no motivation; if he held out no threats, there would be no correction.

"Those who praise you, O Lord, speak of the excellence of your terrible deeds, the greatness of the work of your hands which punish and distribute discipline. They shall speak and will not remain silent. They will not proclaim your everlasting kingdom and silence your everlasting fire. For it is the praise of God that sets you on your way that ought to show you both what you should love and what you should fear; what you should seek, and what you should shun; what you should choose, and what you should reject. The time to choose is now. The time of reward is later. Let the excellence of your terrible things be proclaimed now. Although it is endless, so, too, your greatness has no end, and they shall not be silent about it. How shall they tell of it if it has no end? They shall proclaim it with their praise; and because there is no end of it, so, too, there will be no end to his praise."[129]

Chapter 15

Prayer of Adoration

45. What is adoration?

"You have told me already, Lord; my interior ear has heard a loud voice saying that you are eternal, the only One to possess immortality, because your form does not change nor are you moved. Your will does not alter with the passing of ages; while lacking immortality, a will desires this now, and something else later.

"Then you told me, Lord, with a strong voice in my interior ear, that all existing natures and substances, unlike you, have been made by you. Only 'nothing' comes not from you, and the separation of one's will from you who are Being itself, choosing lesser beings. Such separation is a crime. It is a sin."[130]

"Then you said to me with a strong interior voice, that even a creature who desires you alone is not eternal as are you. Yet in persevering chastity one draws his strength from you and then, in no way shows himself to be changeable. For you are always present to him and he ever makes you the object of his affection, thus keeping himself (in a permanent present) with no future to look forward to or past to remember, undergoing no change or worldly distraction. O blessed is he, if such a one exists, who cleaves to your blessedness. Blessed is he in you, his eternal Inhabitant and Enlightener."[131]

In these reflections, St. Augustine shows us the way to adore God. Adoration is recognition of God as Creator, and all creatures with intellects and wills (angels and men) are bound to adore God. From this recognition comes the sense for the sacred — that awareness that there is something transcendent upon which we are dependent, something worthy of our veneration. This expresses itself in the virtue of religion — that universal awareness that man has that he is indebted to a Supreme Being. Religion takes the form of adoration and sacrifice. Augustine shows us how our adoration and sacrifice are perfected in Christ: "All of the redeemed city, that is, the assembled community of the saints, offers itself to God as a universal sacrifice by means of the High Priest."[132]

The perfect sacrifice is Christ's, perpetuated in the sacrifice of the Eucharist. Our adoration and sacrifice come together and are united to Christ's in the form of eucharistic adoration and communion: "Let no one receive the Eucharist without first adoring it. He not only does not sin by adoring it, he sins in not adoring it."[133]

Chapter 16

Prayer of Thanksgiving

46. What is thanksgiving?

"Nothing will be sweeter in heaven than to thank Christ for his Blood by which we have been saved."[134]

Thanksgiving implies recognition of favors received. Thus, it is an expression that attempts to pay back, if only in word, the benefactor who has gratuitously and generously given of himself.

"*How can I repay the Lord for all the good done for me* (Ps. 116:12) for even as my memory recalls these things, my soul is not repulsed by them? I will love you, O Lord, and thank you, and profess your name, because you have taken from me these evil and reprehensible deeds of mine.

"I attribute it to your grace and to your mercy, that you have melted my sins like so much ice. I attribute to your grace also the evil I did not commit, for what was I capable of doing, loving sin for the sake of sin? Yes, I confess that you have forgiven me what I have committed through maliciousness and what I did not commit, thanks to your guidance."[135]

After recognizing the gifts received, gratitude praises with thanksgiving, and then sets out to give something back. To God who has everything, we give him what only we can give him: our hearts and our tireless service for his glory.

"Thanks be to God! Is there something better we could have in our hearts or on our lips, or written by our pens? Thanks be to God! Nothing more easily said, nothing more pleasant to the ear or as profound in meaning, and profitable in practice than this."[136]

Chapter 17

Prayer for Mercy

47. Is God merciful to all who call on Him?

"If you wish to be satisfied with the good things of God, let mercy be satisfied within you."[137]

"See how you are already beginning to unite yourself with him, because you hate what he hates. Sin has to be punished, because the scepter of justice is the scepter of the kingdom. But could sin go unpunished? It cannot. Sin has to be punished, because if it did not have to be punished, it would no longer be sin. Prevent this from happening; if you do not want to be punished by him, punish yourself."[138]

"It is necessary that for every injustice, great or small, punishment follow — either by the man himself who repents, or by God who distributes justice. Further, he who repents is already punishing himself. Therefore, brethren, let us punish our own sins if we want to obtain God's mercy. There is no escaping it: either you punish yourself or he will punish you."[139]

Placing oneself in God's presence prepares the soul better to assess and recognize its state. Simon Peter, upon recognizing Jesus' divinity, immediately realized his own sinful state: *Leave me, Lord, I am a sinful man* (Luke 5:8). The prayer for mercy is a recognition not only of God's utter holiness but also of one's culpability and willed dissimilarity to God. This prayer asks for forgiveness while one's desire for God expiates the effects of sin on the human heart.

The need for punishment for sin explains the mystery of the sacrifice of the Cross. Man has offended the infinitely good God, thus committing a quasi-infinite offense. No man, nor all men together, could make reparation for such an offense. Only a divine Victim could adequately repair the rift between God and man — but, out of justice, it must be a man who pays the price; hence, the Incarnation and Cross of our Lord. Thanks to the merits of Christ's Cross, we can unite our prayers and sacrifices to the one efficacious sacrifice offered by Christ. The sacrifice of the Mass renews the effects of Christ's sacrifice for sin.

In the Eucharist, says St. Augustine, the most perfect sacrifice and the most perfect prayer of reparation are offered by Christ, who "prays for us, prays in us, and is prayed to by us."[140] "In the sacrament of the altar (the Church) teaches us that . . . she offers us herself."[141]

"Consider well, brethren, what good things God gives to sinners — and then learn what he gives to his servants. To those sinners who blaspheme him every day, he gives the sky and the earth, he gives springs, fruit, health, children, wealth, bounty. All these good things God alone can give. If he gives such as this to sinners, what must he have reserved for his faithful ones? No, not the earth, but heaven. But perhaps with 'heaven' I understate it; for he gives himself who made heaven. Heaven is beautiful, but even more beautiful is its Maker."[142]

48. Who should pray for mercy?

"Everyone has need of remission of sins."[143] "The righteous also should pay to obtain the remission of sins."[144] "The saint can pray only because God has forgiven him his sins."[145] Therefore, if we would only recognize our sins, we would find their remedy in prayer.[146]

Chapter 18

Prayer of Petition

49. What is prayer of petition?

Prayer of petition is born of the awareness of our need. But the mere fact that we ask God for things speaks not only of our indigence but also of his ability and disposition to grant what we ask. Indeed, Christ assures us of this: *Ask and you shall receive, seek and you shall find, knock and it will opened to you* (Matt. 7:7). St. Augustine takes up this theme saying, that God "has every intention of giving, but only to him who asks, so as not to give something to one who would refuse to take it."[147] Therefore, "we have no other hope than that of having confidence in our petitioning knock."[148]

Nonetheless, we are confronted with some problems in all of this. Does our petitioning inform him of what he does not know? — for he is omniscient. Does our asking change his will? In the next few chapters Augustine tackles these questions with the mental agility of a genius and the heart of a pastor of souls.

50. Is prayer of petition necessary if before we ask him, he knows what we need?

"This would cause our minds consternation if we did not understand that the Lord our God requires us to ask him — not that he discovers what our wishes are, for it cannot be unknown to him

— but that through our prayer, the petitions made in us bring about the proper dispositions of desire with which we ought to receive whatever he grants us. His gifts are indeed great, yet we are petty and ungracious in receiving. Thus, we are told, *Do not harness yourselves in an uneven team of unbelievers* (2 Cor. 6:14). Because in proportion to the simplicity of our faith, the determination of our hope, and the passion of our desire, we will better receive that which is immensely great, which *eye has not seen*, because it has no color; which *ear has not heard*, because it has not sound; and which has not entered into the heart of man, because the heart of man has to ascend to it (cf. 1 Cor. 2:9)."[149]

"We need words, therefore, so that in using them, we are helped to consider what it is we ask for — not in order to inform God or move him to comply."[150]

Augustine says elsewhere that God, who is all good, wants us to ask of him good things: "If you would be good, ask God to make you good. But there is another good by which you can do good, and that is whatever good you possess."[151] And in doing so, we grow in confidence in him. "Therefore, if you want to be righteous, be God's beggar, since he just exhorted us in today's Gospel to ask, to seek, to knock . . . he exhorts you to ask. Will he refuse you what you ask?"[152]

"How much more will the Good One give who commands us to ask and is displeased when we do not ask? Even when he gives slowly, it is to show us the value of his good things — he is not refusing us them. Those things which we have desired for a long time are gotten with great pleasure, whereas those things which came easily are held in disdain. So, seek, ask quickly. Because by your seeking and asking you will grow in order to receive more. God reserves for you what he does not want to give you quickly, so that you learn to long with great desire for the best of things. Thus, we should *pray without ceasing*."[153]

51. What about those who do not know to pray for themselves? Are they lost?

The ability and the desire to pray are gifts from God, and they are given to everyone in different degrees. It is written on our nature that we should seek God and speak to him. Nonetheless, we find many who claim they do not. And still others claim they will not. But "there are gifts that God gives even to those who do not pray, such as the birth of faith. And there are gifts that God gives only to those who pray, such as final perseverance."[154]

52. What makes our prayer of petition more efficacious?

St. Augustine cites Sacred Scripture, his perennial source of inspiration, for the answer to this. In this passage, he is asking for prayer of intercession for himself and instructs Proba, the recipient of the letter, how to get the best results.

"By all means, pray for me in earnest. I would not want your deference for the high office I hold, one replete with dangers, to defer from giving me the help I know I need so much. The family of Christ [the Church] prayed for Peter and Paul. And I rejoice that you are in that family, for I need prayers exceedingly more than Peter and Paul ever needed the help of the brethren. With one heart, imitate each other in a holy rivalry, because you struggle not with each other, but with the Devil, common enemy of all the saints.

"*By fasting, long watches, and every type of mortification of the body, prayer is supported* (Tob. 12:8). Each should do what she can. If someone is incapable of doing something, let another take it upon herself, and she will accomplish it through that other one . . . The one who can accomplish less should not hold the others back. The one who can accomplish more should not lord it over those who cannot. Your conscience is responsible before God — you owe nothing to each other except mutual love. May the Lord who can do all we can ask or imagine hear your prayers."[155]

Although our fasting, mortification, and vigils are helpful — indeed, necessary — "God has ordained that we fight more with prayer than with our own efforts."[156] So, "strive in prayer to be victorious in overcoming this world. Pray with hope, pray with faith and love. Pray with perseverance and patience."[157]

53. How can we receive what God bestows graciously?

It's important to recognize that not only the pleasant things are his blessings. "When Christ our Lord has come and dwelt in the soul by faith, and has promised yet another light, and has inspired and given patience, and has warned the man not to delight in prosperity or be crushed by adversity, the faith-filled man begins to treat this world with indifference. Suddenly he is not lifted up when prosperity comes his way, nor is he crushed under adversity, but he learns to praise God in all things — when he is rich and when he is in poverty, in health and sickness, in such a way that the hymn is truly his, *I will bless the Lord at all times; his praise shall be ever in my mouth* (Ps. 23:2). Therefore, to answer the question, we should receive it all with God's praise in our mouth, regardless of the nature of the gift, because we praise the Giver, not the gift."[159]

Chapter 19

What to Ask For

54. If God wants us to ask him for what we need, what precisely *is* it that we need?

First, we should recognize who it is we pray to — a providential and loving Father — and then what it is we pray for — "those things which it is our duty to ask for we should not hesitate to ask, neither for ourselves, for our friends and strangers and yes, even for enemies."[160] But what precisely those things are has been laid out for us by Christ himself: "If we pray correctly, according to our needs, we pray for nothing except that which makes up the Lord's Prayer. And whoever prays for anything not contained in the Lord's Prayer, prays in such a way that is either improper or, at least, unspiritual."[161]

55. What does "hallowed be thy name" mean?

"When praying 'hallowed be thy name,' we remind ourselves to aspire to make God's ever-holy name held as holy by all men. In other words, not scorned, which in any account is more an advantage for men than for God."[162] For example, when someone prays, *As in their sight you have proved yourself holy before us*, *so now in our sight prove yourself great before them*, and *let your prophets be proved worthy of belief* (Ecclus. 36:4,18), what else does he pray for than "hallowed be thy name"?[163]

In other words, this petition is multiform, including diverse manners in which God's name is held holy — above all in reverence before God and personal holiness. It may seem that this petition overlaps somewhat with "thy kingdom come," but that is not a problem, as long as these petitions are heard and we know how to cooperate with God's grace!

St. Augustine counsels praying to keep God's name holy in our lives by asking for:

- Pure love: ". . . but in those from whom love is requited in a holy and pure way, we understandably find true delight. For these things, it is fitting that we pray: if we have them, that we may retain them; if we do not have them, that we may obtain them";[164]
- Continence;
- Fidelity in marriage;
- Fidelity of priests to their vocation;
- The flock of believers;[165]
- Preachers and teachers of the Faith;[166]
- Perseverance in good proposals;[167]
- Spiritual progress.[168]

56. What does "thy kingdom come" mean?

"When we say, 'Thy kingdom come' — which indubitably shall come whether we desire it or not — we arouse our own desire for that kingdom by saying these words. We pray that it come to us, and that we be deemed worthy to reign in it."[169]

"If we love Christ, then certainly, we ought to long for his coming. It is completely wrong and I doubt whether it is really possible to fear the arrival of him whom you love or to pray 'Thy kingdom come,' and to fear that your prayer be heard. Who is coming to judge you but the One who came to be judged for your sake?"[170]

"The coming of the Lord is not loved by anyone who says it is close at hand or very far off, but by him who, be it far or near, looks forward to it with sincere faith, firm hope, and ardent charity."[171]

When someone prays, *Do not hold past iniquities against us; may your compassion come quickly, for we have been brought very low* (Ps. 79:7), what else does he say than "Thy kingdom come"?[172]

Other ways of praying for the coming of the kingdom, which is within us, are to ask for the following:

- God's blessings in the form of his providence;
- The gift of prayer;[173]
- True happiness and fulfillment;
- God's tenderness;
- Faith;[174]
- All the theological virtues (faith, hope, and charity);[175]
- Wisdom;[176]
- Intelligence;[177]
- To become what we should be;[178]
- That Jesus reveal his Face;[179]
- The Holy Spirit;[180]
- To be saved.[181]

57. What does "Thy will be done" mean?

"When we pray, 'Thy will be done on earth as it is in heaven,' we pray for ourselves that he give us the grace of obedience, that his will be done by us just as it is done by his angels in heaven."[182]

"When someone prays, *Direct my steps as you have promised, let evil win no power over me* (Ps. 119:133), what else does he pray for than, 'Thy will be done on earth as it is in heaven'?"[183]

It seems that God desires our cooperation with his will so that his plans will come to fruition with our consent. St. Augustine suggests other ways of praying for God's will to be done by asking:

- For docility to the Holy Spirit;[184]
- To obey God's law;[185]
- To fulfill duty;[186]
- To obtain justice;
- For what we do not know we need, but what God knows to be our need;[187]
- To make us good.[188]

58. What does "give us this day our daily bread" mean?

"When we pray, 'Give us this day our daily bread,' the word 'this day' means this present time, in which we ask for all that makes up temporal blessings, which I have discussed previously; and 'bread' means the sacrament of believers, which in this present time is necessary in order to obtain the felicity — not in the present time — but in eternity."[189]

"When someone prays, *Give me neither poverty nor riches*, what else does he pray for than, 'Give us this day our daily bread'?"[190]

Other ways of praying for temporal blessings in the order of eternal life are asking for the following:

- A happy life;[191]
- To conserve life;[192]
- To understand Sacred Scripture;[193]
- Spiritual well-being, more than physical;
- A wealth of eternal goods, and a moderate degree of temporal goods.[194]

59. What does "forgive us our trespasses as we forgive those who trespass against us" mean?

"When we pray, 'Forgive us our sins as we forgive those who trespass against us,' we are reminded of both what we should ask, and what we should do in order to be worthy of receiving what we ask."[195]

"When someone prays, *Lord, remember David and all his anxious care* (Ps. 132:1), or *Lord my God, if I am at fault in this, if there is guilt on my hands, if I have repaid my friend with evil* (Ps. 7:3), what else does he pray for than, 'Forgive us our trespasses as we forgive those who trespass against us'?"[196]

Other ways of making this same petition are by asking for:

- Evil to be taken away and good put in its place;[197]
- Remission of sins;[198]
- Deliverance from hidden faults;[199]
- Forgiveness and conversion of our enemies;[200]
- An enemy to be lost and a friend gained;[201]
- Repentance.[202]

"Endure, for this you were born. Endure, because perhaps you are endured. If you have always been good, be merciful. If at any time you were evil, do not forget it. But who is always good? If God should carefully sift you, he will most likely find you more evil than you think yourself good . . . The gathering of the crop in the field will come to an end and the separation of the harvest will follow."[203]

"If you would obtain mercy, be merciful. If you are not humane to men, though you are a man, God will deny you divinity, that is the incorruption of immortality, by which he makes us gods. For God needs nothing from you, but you need God. He seeks nothing from you to be blessed, but unless you receive him, you cannot be blessed . . . But he will not give you anything of those things which he has created except himself, the Creator of all things, that you may enjoy him. And how will he do this? Do you think you deserve it? If you were to seek what you deserve, he would give you back your sins. If you sought recompense for your sins, what would befall you but death? Have pity on man, O man, and God will have pity on you. You and your neighbor, both men, are pitiable creatures. But God is not pitiable; rather he has a pitying heart."[204]

60. What does "lead us not into temptation" mean?

"When we pray, 'Lead us not into temptation,' we remind ourselves to seek that we may not, through being deprived of God's help, be either compelled to consent or enmeshed in temptation."[205]

"When someone prays, *Do not let lechery and lust grip me, do not give me over to shameless desire* (Ecclus. 23:6), what else does he pray for than, 'Lead us not into temptation'?"[206]

Other ways of praying not to be led into temptation are to ask:

- For integrity;
- To resist in time of tribulation;[207]
- To overcome pride;[208]
- To eliminate vice;[209]
- To resist concupiscence.[210]

"Temptation comes about like a sort of inquiry in which man discovers who he is, for previously, he was hidden from himself, but not so hidden from his Maker. Peter presumed to have something he did not yet have, that he would persevere with our Lord unto death. Peter did not know his own strength, but our Lord did. Temptation came. He denied Jesus. And weeping, he received the strength (Luke 22:33-62). Since, therefore, we do not know what we should ask for, even when we have it, nor give thanks even when we receive, we should be educated in this world by trial and temptation."[211]

61. What does "deliver us from evil" mean?

"When we pray, 'Deliver us from evil,' we tell ourselves to consider that we do not yet enjoy that good estate in which we experience no evil. And this petition, which comes last in the Lord's

Prayer, is so comprehensive that a Christian, regardless of the trial he finds himself in, can use it in his groans and find release in tears. He can start with this petition, and continue with it until the conclusion of his prayer. It is necessary that these words and all that they mean should be kept fresh in our memory.[212]

"What else can it be than, 'Lead us not into temptation' when someone prays, *Rescue me from my enemies, my God, protect me from those attacking me* (Ps. 59:1). Review all the words of every holy prayer. I think you will find nothing but that which comprises the Lord's Prayer. When praying, we are at liberty to use different words to any degree, but we must ask the same things. In this we have no other option."[213]

Other ways of asking for this very same grace are to pray:

- To overcome sin in all of its forms;[214]
- To be freed from enemies;[215]
- For sinners and the errant;[216]
- For salvation;[217]
- For those we must correct;[218]
- For protection against the Devil;[219]
- For spiritual protection in times of persecution;[220]
- For defense against sinful neglect;
- For patience and meekness;
- To overcome bad habits;[221]
- To resist an attraction to evil[222]
- For freedom.[223]

62. If St. Augustine can give such an exhaustive list of things to pray for, why does St. Paul say that *we do not know what to pray for as we ought* (cf. Rom. 8:26)?

"Perhaps you may still ask why the apostle said, 'We know not what to pray for as we ought,' for it is completely unbelievable that he or those to whom he wrote did not know the Lord's Prayer. He was not unthinking or wrong when he wrote that. So what, then, can we make of that statement? Is it not true that our trials and difficulties are, for the great part, useful in curbing our pride, or for testing and exercising our patience? For we know that after such tribulation and correction, either a great reward or the punishment and the purification of sins awaits us. But, nonetheless, are we not ignorant of what good purpose these things could serve, wishing to be freed from them?

"The apostle shows that even he was not oblivious to this. In fact, in order that he not be swelled with pride, given the exalted nature of his revelations, a thorn in the flesh was given him, a messenger from Satan was sent to beat him. Not knowing exactly what to pray for, he begged the Lord three times to take it from him. In time, he received God's answer, explaining why a man of such advanced prayer was denied what he asked for, and why it was more appropriate that it not be taken from him: *My grace is enough for you; my power is at its best in weakness* (2 Cor. 12:7-9)."[224]

63. What can we be assured of receiving, knowing not only that God will grant it, but that it will be for the best?

"Whoever desires from the Lord that 'one thing,' and seeks after it (Ps. 27:4), asks with certainty and trust, without fearing that, once he receives it, it would do him harm and without which everything else that he may have obtained by asking for it in the right way would be useless to him. I am referring to the only true and happy life, in which we, in immortal and incorruptible body and spirit, eternally contemplate the joy of the Lord. Everything else is asked for in the right way and desired if in view of this one thing. Whoever possesses it possesses all he could want and, having it, could not desire anything else which would be improper. For it contains the spring of life which we thirst for in our prayer as long as we hope, even as we are deprived of seeing that for which we hope. Confident, under the shadow of his wings with our desire placed before him, we will be completely satisfied with the riches of his house. We will be made to drink of the river of his delights, since with him the spring of life becomes truly a living spring. And in his light we shall see the light, when our desire shall be satisfied with every good thing, where there shall be nothing else to long for with our groaning, but rejoicing we shall possess all.

"Further, since his blessing is nothing less than the *peace of God which is so much greater than we can understand* (Phil. 4:7), even when we ask for it in prayer, we do not know for what we are asking. Since we cannot imagine it as it really is, we do not know what it is, and whatever form we come up with in our minds is to be rejected, cast away, and condemned. We know that it is not what we seek, yet we do not know enough about it to say exactly what it is that we seek."[225]

64. What about those prayers for interior gifts — how can I know that God has answered such prayers?

Augustine speaks of an interior knowledge born of love and trust in God that assures an answer to prayers for interior gifts. It is a *knowledge beyond all knowing* (Eph. 3:19), an inner conviction that assures the man of prayer of God's generous answer. While this is indemonstrable to others, the contemplative soul who has experienced God's presence knows who it is that he has experienced.

"*For behold, God helps me*, for they do not know in whom I hide. If they were to turn to God, they know in what way God is my helper. All holy men are helped by God interiorly, where no one can see. Just as the conscience of evil men is their great chastisement, so, too, is the conscience of holy men a great joy. The apostle says, *For our boast is this, the testimony of our conscience that we have conducted ourselves in the world, and especially toward you, with the simplicity and sincerity of God, (and) not by human wisdom but by the grace of* God (2 Cor. 1:12). It is in the interior . . . that a man can glory and say, *For behold, God helps me*. Of course, what God promises is still far off, but even today I enjoy his sweet and ever-present help. Today, without apparent cause, I can say with certainty in the joy of my heart, *Offer fitting sacrifice and trust in the Lord. Many say, 'May we see better times! Lord, show us the light of your face!' But you have given my heart more joy than they have when grain and wine abound* (Ps. 4:6-7). Not into my vineyard, not into my flock, not into my cask or into my table, but 'into my heart.' *For behold God helps me*. How does he help me? He elevates my soul."[226]

65. But is receiving what we ask for in this life enough to make us happy?

"But once people have obtained benefits for themselves and for those whom they love, can we truly say that they are now happy? Certainly, they have something desirable, but if they have not other things still greater, better, and more useful and beautiful, they still fall short of possessing a [perfectly] happy life."[227]

66. Does God hear some people's prayers more than others?

Augustine seems to think that God has a certain weakness toward some people that he does not show to everyone — above all to those who suffer, and widows in particular. Perhaps foreseeing Mary's widowhood, our Lord has chosen to keep widows closest to him.

"God has taught us that prayer is every member's duty (that is, those who believe in him and are united to his Body). Nonetheless, in the Scriptures, a more attentive prayer is expected of widows. In fact, there are two women named Anna mentioned with distinction — the one, Elkanah's wife, who was the mother of holy Samuel; the other, the widow who recognized the most holy One when [he was] still an infant. The first one, although married, prayed with a broken heart and a heavy mind because she had no sons. Once she received Samuel, she consecrated him to the Lord to fulfil the vow made when she prayed for a son. Although it is not easy to say under which petition of the Lord's Prayer this falls, it could be under the last, 'deliver us from evil,' since it was considered evil to be married and not to have children as the fruit of marriage.

"Take note of what is written about the other widow, Anna: *She never left the temple, serving God night and day with fasting and prayer* (Luke 2:36-37). Similarly, as quoted earlier, the apostle said, *But a woman who is really widowed and left without anybody can give herself up to God and consecrate all her days and nights to petitions and prayer* (1 Tim. 5:5). And the Lord, when counseling men to pray always and not to weaken, used the example of a widow who importunately persevered and persuaded the judge to hear her case, even though he was unjust and evil, a man who feared neither God nor men. How pressing it is, then, to outdo others in devoting time to prayer is clearly seen by the fact that the exhortations to earnest and persevering prayer are made using examples of widows."[228]

67. In other words, the bereaving and those who feel abandoned have a special place in God's Heart?

If God lays such importance on the prayers of widows and widowers, they most surely have an important role to play in the economy of salvation.

"What makes this task especially suitable for widows is precisely their bereaved and desolate state. For whoever understands that he is in this world as a bereaving and desolate pilgrim far from the Lord will be careful to dedicate his widowhood to God, as it were, who is his protector in constant and fervent prayer. So pray, therefore, as a widow who belongs to Christ, although you do not yet see him, but imploring nonetheless his help. Although you are quite wealthy, pray as a poor person, since your true riches of the coming world are not yet in your possession — but have no fear of their loss . . . the more piously you order your house, the more likely are you to persevere in fervent prayer, not mixing in the affairs of this world beyond their interest for the spiritual life."[229]

68. Is it all right to pray for our own honors and acquiring power, and might we pray that others achieve such things?

"Might we say, then, that in addition to bodily health, men might desire honor and power for themselves and for loved ones? Certainly, if they desire them in order to promote the common interest of those dependent upon them. If they seek these things not as ends in themselves, but for some good thing accomplished through these means, their desire is proper. But if they simply want to gratify their pride and arrogance, a superficial and harmful victory for their vanity, then their wish is improper."[230]

69. Why are some people's prayers not answered?

• *Perhaps we ask in a bad way — with distractions, for example.* Augustine offers some consoling advice for those who are distracted in prayer. "*For you, Lord, are good and gracious . . . prayers are often frustrated by vain thoughts, as when one's heart is hardly turned to God in prayer . . . Each one of us has had this experience, but probably would not think that it happens to others as well were we not to find it in the Sacred Scriptures, where David says, since I have found my heart, O Lord, in order to pray to you*. He said that he 'found his heart' as if it were something used to escaping him, and he had to pursue it like a fugitive, unable to catch it and crying out to God, 'My heart has abandoned me.' Therefore, my brethren, considering what he says in this passage, I believe I know what he means when he says 'gracious.' It seems that he calls God gracious because he expects prayers from us but bears our weakness, with a view to perfecting us. But when we have given him our prayer, he receives it gratefully and attentively, without giving a thought to those many prayers we pour out thoughtlessly."[231]

• *Sometimes we attempt to manipulate God, turning him into a means to our end.* "Why does Scripture say in many places, *They shall call, but I will not hear them?* . . . and elsewhere, *They have called but not upon God.* They call, but not upon God. You call upon whatever you love. You call upon whatever you call to yourself, whatever you wish to have. Thus, if for this reason you call upon God, asking for money or that an inheritance come your way, that you receive worldly status, you call upon those things that you desire. But you try to make of God the means to your desire, not the listener of your needs."[232]

• *Perhaps God has an even better plan in store.* "God is good if he gives you what you want. But what if what you want is bad? You say, 'I have prayed so much and so often, and still I have not been heard!' Why? What did you pay for? Perhaps for the death of your enemy? What if he were praying for the same for you? He who created you created him, too. You are man, he is a man, but God is the judge. He hears both and grants prayer to neither . . . but what if you say, 'But I didn't ask for that; I didn't ask for the death of my enemy, but for the life of my child. What evil did I pray for?' You prayed for no evil. What if he was taken away *lest wickedness alter his understanding*? 'But he was a sinner, I wanted him to live to be converted.' You wanted him to live, in order that he become better, but what if God knew that he would become worse had he lived longer? If you call on God as God, trust that you shall be heard. You have a place in that verse, *and of great mercy to all who invoke you*."[233]

• *We ask for evil things*. "The apostle James used this as grounds to chastise his flock when he said, *The reason you do not receive what you want . . . it is because you have not prayed properly; you have prayed for something to indulge your own desires* (Jas. 4:3). What someone desires to obtain so as to use it toward an improper end, merciful God refuses to grant."[234]

• *Perhaps we do not see as God sees*. "Why are you sad that your prayers have gone unanswered? Perhaps you ask for something that would not bring you joy . . . It is God's mercy to deny us what we ask if it were to our ruin."[235]

St. Augustine gives an example any parent can understand of a child who wants a sword or wants to ride a horse, but the responsible parent knows that such things contain dangers unknown or little considered by a four-year-old. It is no mean-spirited denial of a petition, but for the best of the one who asks unaware of what would happen were such a request granted.[236]

• *God does not heed the prayers of hypocrites*. "You dwell in a holy place. Therefore, you will not hear the impure words of sin . . . not of him who sought his own praise in tasting the forbidden fruit, who, upon opening his bodily eyes should attempt to hide himself from your sight."[237]

• *When the suffering person's righteous request seems unanswered, confidence in God is counseled*. "He who tends to our needs knows when to give what we need. Why do I say this, brethren? In case anyone weaken because he has not been heard after making a righteous request of God. If he has not been heard, [let him not] be discouraged, [nor] weaken, but let his eyes await the food [God] gives in due season. When [God] does not grant something, it is because it would do some harm."[238]

70. Augustine offers possible explanations for why God does not grant some things. Is there something one *could* ask for with the assurance of receiving it?

In one of his most beautiful passages, Augustine tells us that God gives himself to all who simply ask.

"For what better than God could be given to me? God loves me. God loves you. Look, he has even proposed to you, ask him what you want. If the emperor were to tell you, 'Ask whatever you want,' what posts, what dignities would blurt out of your mouth! What great things would you imagine, both to receive and give away! But when God says to you, 'Ask for whatever you want,' what do you want? Empty your mind, be greedy, stretch out as far as you can, increase your desire. Was it not God who said, 'Ask for whatever you want'? If you are a lover of possessions, you will desire the whole earth and every man your servant or slave. But when you have the whole world in your possession — then what? You will then ask for the sea, yet you cannot live there. The fish will outdo you in greediness there. But perhaps you want islands. Leave them. Ask for the air, but you cannot fly. Stretch your desire unto the heavens, call the sun your own, and the moon and the stars, because he who made it all has said, 'Ask for whatever you want.' Yet you can find no better treasure, nothing better, than him who made all these things. Seek him who made all, and in him and thanks to him you shall have all that he has made. All these things are precious because they are beautiful. But what is more beautiful than he? He would not rather give you anything else than himself. If you have found something better, ask him for it. But know that you do him an injustice and harm to yourself in preferring it over him who made it — when all along he wants to give himself to you."[239]

Chapter 20

What Not to Ask For

71. St. Augustine says God does not answer some of our prayers because we ask for the wrong things. What are those things?

"And so, may it be love alone that remains; for he himself is our fruit. And for the moment this love remains as ardent desire, not yet fulfilled or wholly enjoyed, and whatever it be that we ask in the name of the only-begotten Son will the Father give us. But we should not think that that which does not serve us in the order of salvation could be asked in the Savior's name; for we ask only that which helps along the path of salvation."[240]

Christ taught us to pray in order to teach us how to desire God, how to love him.[241] Given that "prayer is the source of our salvation,"[242] it would be tragic to turn it toward our own downfall, because "to ask for things outside of the blessed life is to ask for nothing."[243] And since we know what we want, but not necessarily what God wants,[244] Augustine helps his entrusted flock to know what not to ask for:

- Worldly honors;[245]
- Wealth;[246]
- The downfall of him who plots against you;[247]
- Temporal joy alone;[248]
- Anything that would incur guilt;[249]

- Anything that would hinder salvation;[250]
- Anything evil.[251]

"I do not think anyone will find anything in these things that matches what is contained in the Lord's Prayer. We should be ashamed if we were to ask for such things, even if we are not ashamed to desire them. But if we should be ashamed that we desire them and, nonetheless, feel the desire for them, how much better would it be if we were to ask to be liberated from this sick desire by him to whom we pray, 'Deliver us from evil'!"[252]

Chapter 21

Praying Always

72. How are we to understand the injunction *pray always*?

Augustine has already told us that God does not demand the impossible from us. But when God does demand something beyond our own capabilities, he is more than willing to help us accomplish it.

"*I will bless the Lord at all times; his praise shall ever be in my mouth*. This is how Christ speaks, and so, too, should the Christian speak; because a Christian is a member of the Body of Christ . . . When should I praise the Lord? . . . In times of great blessing? No; 'at all times.' Therefore, in those moments (of blessing) and when you experience the Lord's scourges, when good things are taken away . . . you have sung, 'I will bless the Lord at all times; his praise will ever be in my mouth,' both when he gives and when he takes away, because it is he who gives and he who takes away, but God will never take himself away from him who blesses God."[253]

73. But who is capable of praying at all times?

The humble man, says St. Augustine, is capable of blessing the Lord at all times.

"How does man bless the Lord at all times? By not seeking praise for himself . . . if you seek humility, repeat what is written, *In the*

Lord shall my soul be praised: the humble shall hear him and rejoice. Be the Lord's donkey, be humble. He who sits on you, rules you. Don't fear getting tripped up or falling head first — for that is the nature of your weakness. Simply consider who it is that rides on you — you carry Christ. He came into the city on a donkey, and that animal was gentle."[254]

Since it is necessary to pray always, but it is impossible to pray in every moment with words, Augustine suggests, "If you sing with the voice, soon you must be silent. In those moments, sing with your life in such a way that your song is never silent."[255] And all of this should be done:

- "With insistence";[256]
- "With perseverance";[257]
- "Without laziness"[258] or "getting discouraged."[259]

74. But when prayer is understood in its narrow sense, how long should it last? How long should I prolong my prayer?

"It is neither illicit nor unprofitable to pray at length, if your time allows for it without conflicting with your obligations and duty-bound work — even in the doing of these things, as I have already said, we should exercise holy desire, which is praying without ceasing."[260]

75. I thought Christ said we shouldn't pray with lots of words. How do we reconcile that with what Augustine says about praying at length?

Spending long periods in prayer is not, as many believe, the same as "praying with lots of words." An accumulation of words is one thing, heartfelt desire extended over long periods is quite another. "It is written that even the Lord himself spent entire nights in prayer, and that his prayer was even with more insistence when he was in agony. In all of this, do we not see the example of our needed Intercessor who is in time, who, with the Father is also the eternal Hearer of prayer?"[261]

76. Since we are encouraged to pray at length and this even vocally when we can, what form does that take?

"The brethren in Egypt, it is said, had recourse to frequent prayers, but they were quite brief — spontaneous maxims, as it were, lest their attentive and alert minds, necessary for prolonged prayer, lose their edge or simply dissipate. Here they show us plainly, that as the attention cannot continue long if fatigued, so, too, it should not be pendant if it is to be maintained. Nor should we use 'lots of words' in our prayer, nor should we avoid prolonged prayer if we have the fervent attention to do so. 'Lots of words' in prayer means speaking too much while asking for what we need. Prolonged prayer means a throbbing heart full of holy sentiments for him to whom we pray. Often, prayer is more groaning than talking, more tears than words. But our tears are not lost on him, and our groaning is ever before him who made the word and has no need of human words."[262]

77. What form does this "desire" take in our prayer?

"When we relish continuous desire, accompanied by the practice of faith, hope, and charity, then we 'pray always.' "[263]

Desire is central for St. Augustine's theology of prayer. He recognizes the constant need to reorient his easily distracted heart toward its true and divine Love, because "if I love all things when I do not possess them, and when I do possess them, I despise them, what good thing, then, can satisfy me?"[264]

"Desire is the soul's thirst";[265] it is "the most intimate portion of the heart."[266] Intimate knowledge of the Beloved reveals his goodness to the man of prayer, and prayer orders and orients his desire toward the Beloved. This makes "the whole of the life of a Christian to be one holy desire, and it is only this that makes us Christians."[267]

78. What are the fruits of this desire in prayer?

"We learn to correct ourselves, we discover what spiritual progress we have made through desire, and we affectionately arouse in our souls the ability to receive even more strength. The effects of prayer will be just as good for the soul as the degree of fervent desire which provoked its expression."[268]

"Desire renders much sweeter what has been desired over much time, once it has been obtained,"[269] "while it capacitates the soul to receive to an even greater degree what it has so ardently longed for. It is not joy that capacitates the soul, but desire."[270]

79. What will help me to achieve this desire?

Regardless of our circumstances, direct contact with Sacred Scripture helps us keep our focus.

"As pilgrims, distant from the Lord, we walk in the obscurity of this world. Since *we walk by faith, not sight* (cf. 2 Cor. 5:6), the Christian soul should experience desolation, continuing in prayer and learning to set his eye on the word of divine Sacred Scripture, as on a light shining in a dark place, until the day dawns, and the day-star arises in our hearts . . . and *we know that when it shall be revealed, we shall be like him, because we shall see him as he is* (1 John 3:2). For after death comes the true life, and after desolation, true consolation. That life shall free our 'souls from death'; that consolation shall free our 'eyes from tears,' and, as the psalm continues, our 'feet shall be saved from falling'; for there shall be no temptation there."[271]

80. Given the all-important role of desire in prayer, should we conclude that prayer regimens and fixed prayer times constrict our desire?

"The words of the Lord, in fact, *pray without ceasing*, and the apostle, *pray without interruption*, are reasonably understood in the sense that on no given day should the established prayer times be omitted."[272] "Men pray every day, the saints never abandon the time and place reserved for prayer."[273]

Augustine marks out the usual times for prayer as follows:

- After the cock crows (although really fervent souls have already begun their prayer before that);[274]
- When the bread is blessed and consecrated (morning Mass);[275]
- Before lunch;[276]
- More often during Lent.[277]

Chapter 22

Christ's Role in Our Prayer

81. What does Christ have to do with our prayer life?

"God could not have given men a greater gift than making his Word — through whom he created all things — to be their Head, and joining them as members to him, so that the Son of God should also become the Son of Man: one with the Father and with men. In this way, when we pray to God asking for mercy, we do not separate the Son from him. And when the Body of the Son prays, the Head is not separated from itself. For it is one Savior of one Body, our Lord Jesus Christ, the Son of God, who both prays for us, prays in us, and is prayed to by us. As Priest, he prays for us. As Head, he prays in us. As God, he is prayed to by us. We should, then, recognize him in our words and his words in us."[278]

82. What does it mean to say that Christ is Head of the Mystical Body, and how does this play out in our prayer life?

"Inasmuch as he is God, he is prayed to; inasmuch as he is a servant, he prays: at once Creator and created. He takes the creature upon himself and remains unchanged, that the creature might be changed, thus making himself one with us into one Man, Head and Body. Thus, we pray to him, through him, in him. Just so, we speak with him, and he speaks with us. We speak in him, he speaks in us the prayer of the psalm, called 'the Prayer of David'; since our Lord was, in the order of flesh, the son of David; but according to the order of his divine nature, he is the Lord and Creator of David . . . No one, upon hearing these words, therefore, should say that 'Christ does not speak'; nor, too, should anyone utter, 'Nor do I speak'. On the contrary, if he claims to speak in the Body of Christ, he should say both: 'Christ speaks,' and 'I speak.' Desire not to say anything without him or that he say anything without you . . ."[279]

With regard to Christ's relationship to the members of his Mystical Body, Augustine says, "It is one Man who reaches to the end of the world: some members of Christ cry out, while other members rest in him already. Still others cry, while others will cry only when they have had rest, and when they have done, others will cry. For it is the entire Body of Christ whose voice he hears, which says, *I have cried to you all day long*. At the right hand of the Father, our Head intercedes for us: some he recovers, others he punishes; some he purifies, to others he gives comfort; some he is creating, others calling or recalling; some correcting, others restoring."[280]

83. Does that mean that with Christ as the Head, when we pray, Christ prays through us in such a way that we become his mouthpiece?

"In this Psalm [Ps. 131], God's servant's humility and fidelity are commended to us in a song whose voice is the whole Body of Christ. Frequently we have admonished you, beloved, that such as that should not be heard as merely the voice of a singing man, but as the voice of all who form Christ's Body. And since they all make up that Body, one man does indeed speak: he who is one is also many . . . Now he prays in God's temple who prays in the Church's peace, in the unity of the Body of Christ, which is made up of the many throughout the world who believe."[281]

To ensure that it is Christ who prays, we have to sublimate our own egoism and be humble before the Lord and others. Augustine goes on to say, "*Lord, my heart is not lifted up*. He has offered a sacrifice. How do we show that he has offered a sacrifice? Humility of heart is a sacrifice . . . Without a sacrifice there is no priest. Yet we have our High Priest in heaven, and he intercedes for us before the Father . . . Because we have a priest we are safe. There let us offer our sacrifice. But what sort of sacrifice ought we to offer, given that God desires no holocausts as you have surely heard in the psalm? It is precisely there that that he shows us: *The sacrifice that pleases God is an afflicted spirit; a broken, contrite heart, O God, you will not reject*."[282]

84. If we are Christ's mouthpiece when we pray, could we say that when we praise Christ, Christ praises himself?

That is a logical conclusion. But St. Augustine goes one step further. He says that when Christ prayed the psalms which praised David, "it was Christ in the order of human nature as son of David, praising his own divine nature in the God-Man. The title is 'Praise to David himself.' And since he is also called David because he is of the seed of David and is nonetheless our ruling King who brings us into the Kingdom, therefore, 'Praise to David himself' is understood to mean praise to Christ himself. Christ, in the order of flesh is David, as son of David, but in the order of divinity he is David's Creator and Lord: *I will exalt you, my King; I will bless your name now and for all ages*."[283]

85. If Christ's praise is perfect, how does our praise add anything to it?

Rather than add something to Christ's perfect praise, we join it. "*Great is the Lord and very much to be praised* . . . How vast a conception has he included by saying 'very much'? Imagine whatever you want, for how can that which cannot be contained be imagined? *He is very much to be praised. And of his greatness there is no end.* Thus he says 'very much' in case you choose to begin to praise him and then believe to have praised him enough, he whose greatness has no end. Do not think that he whose greatness has no end can ever be praised enough by you. Is it not better, then, that since he has no end, so your praise, too, should have no end? His greatness is endless, let your praise be without end, too."[284]

86. Does this mean that Christ intercedes for us as well or does he only praise himself when we praise him?

"Note John's own humility. Doubtless he was a righteous and great man, who drank in the Lord's mysteries from his bosom. Such is the man who, having drunk from the Lord's side, proclaimed his divinity: *in the beginning was the Word, and the Word was with God.* And such is the man who does not say 'you have an advocate before the Father,' but *if any man sin,* he continues, *we have an advocate.* He does not say 'you have,' nor 'you have me,' nor 'you have Christ himself,' but mentioning Christ he says *we have*, not 'you have.' He numbers himself amongst the sinners so that he, too, might have Christ as an Advocate, rather than having himself as advocate in Christ's place, thus finding himself numbered amongst the proud who are condemned. Brothers, Jesus Christ, the righteous one, is the one we have as our advocate before the Father. 'He,' yes he, 'is the sacrifice for our sins . . .' The apostle prays for the people, the people pray for the apostle. We pray for you, dear brothers, but pray for us, too. Let all the members pray for each other, but let the Head intercede for all . . . Behold, *Christ is the sacrifice for our sins; not only ours, but also those of the entire world.*"[285]

87. Doesn't Christ say, *Anything you ask the Father in my name he will give you?* How does that work?

"We must now take up those words of our Lord: *Anything you ask the Father in my name he will give you*. In previous portions of this discourse of our Lord, with regard to those people who ask certain things of the Father in Christ's name yet do not receive, it has already been said that nothing can be asked of the Father in the Savior's name that is not in conformity to the design of salvation . . . In other words, one who conceives of Christ in such a way that is unfitting of the Son of God does not ask in his name, regardless of whether he not omit the mention of Christ with its syllables and letters . . . But he who considers Christ correctly and asks in his name, receives what he has asked so long as it is not in conflict with his own eternal salvation. Further, he receives it when he should receive it. Some things are not denied, only slow in coming, being granted at the correct time."[286]

88. Christ says, *If you abide in me and my words abide in you, you shall ask whatever you want and it shall be done for you.* What does it mean to abide in Christ?

"Abiding in Christ, could there be anything they might wish for that would be disagreeable to Christ? Abiding in the Savior, could there be anything in their desire in conflict with salvation? We desire certain things because we are in Christ and still other things because we are still in this world. Sometimes, with relation to this present dwelling-place, we can be interiorly urged to ask for something, unaware that it would be to our detriment to receive it. God forbid that we would receive such a thing if we abide in Christ, who, when asked, only does what is to our benefit. Abiding in him, when his words abide in us, we will indeed ask whatever we will and it shall be granted us. If we ask and it comes to nothing, what we asked for did not serve our abiding in him, nor with his words which abide in us, but on the contrary, with the urges and baseness of the flesh which are not in him and do not have his words abiding in them. The prayer he taught us pertains to his words, with which we say, 'Our Father, who art in heaven.' We should be cautioned not to fall away from the words and the meaning of this prayer in our petitions, and whatsoever we ask will be granted to us. Only when we do what he commanded us and love what he promised can we truly say that his words abide in us.

"But should his words abide merely in our memory, lacking a place in our lives, then the branch is separated from the vine because its life does not come from the root. Hence Scripture distinguishes *those who remember his commandments and do them*. For many keep the memory of them yet treat them with contempt, or even mock and revile them. The words of Christ do not abide in those who have some sort of contact but no real connection. And for them, his words will not be a blessing, but their accuser. And since they are present in them without abiding in them, they are held bound to them in order to be judged by them in the end."[287]

Chapter 23

Action and Contemplation

89. Isn't there a conflict between action and contemplation, between our daily banalities and work and the sublime nature of prayer?

After St. Augustine's conversion, he decided to live solely for God. "Now I love you alone . . . I am ready to serve you alone."[288] In following Christ and ultimately accepting the role of bishop, albeit with much concern about his own ability to fulfill that office, Augustine learned to manage his time of work and prayer in such a way that they were not in conflict with each other. In fact, since he was obeying the Church by accepting the burden of being a bishop, he knew that there could be no conflict. He was certain that he was fulfilling God's will.[289]

He mastered the art of time management, protecting his prayer-time with zeal. "Love of truth seeks pious recreation of leisure, while love's demands take up duty out of justice. If such a burden is not imposed, then one should spend time in search and perception of truth. But in this case, delight in the truth should never be abandoned altogether, or its sweet taste will dissipate and duty will become oppression."[290]

That was Augustine's general rule: contemplative search for God without neglecting the demands of justice and charity toward neighbor and society. More precisely, though, the Bishop of Hippo distinguishes three styles of life with their respective degrees of contemplation and work: "Regarding the three kinds of life: contemplative, active, and active-contemplative, although a man may live a life of unimpaired faith and attain to the eternal reward in any one of them, there is a difference between what is held for love of the truth and what is expended in the duty of charity. One may not be so surrendered to contemplation that he neglects caring for his neighbor, nor so given over to the active life, that he never contemplates God . . . The love of truth requires holy repose, and the requirements of charity rightful employment."[291]

"Man's mind has been offered a few talents. One is active, while the other is contemplative: one by which man takes to the path, the other by which man reaches the goal; the one with which man works so that his heart be purified in order to see God, and the other by which man disengages himself in order to see God. The first talent has to do with the laws of behavior in his temporal life, the second, with the law which regards eternal life. Thus, one works while the other rests, since the first brings about the purgation of sins, and the second moves about in the light purgation brings. Just as the one is employed in the work of good conversation, so, too, the other subsists in faith, is witnessed by only a few, *through a glass darkly*, and only partially in a sort of vision of unchanging truth.

"These two talents are represented by the two wives of Jacob . . . *Leah* is translated as 'working,' while *Rachel* means 'the first seen principle.' And this helps us understand, if we pay close attention, that the three Gospel writers, with unsurpassed richness, have treated our Lord's temporal affairs as well as his sayings, which were primarily meant to orient and shape our affairs in this present life, by stressing this talent. Yet John narrates far fewer of the

Lord's doings; rather, he reports the greater treasury of the words he spoke with more accuracy. Above all, he concentrates on those things that would bring us to the knowledge of the Trinity and the beatitude of eternal life. To this end, he laid it all out by stressing the contemplative talent.[292]

"Clearly, both action and contemplation are necessary so long as we are in this world. No one will deny that. He frequently refers to Martha and Mary, the sisters of Lazarus, as the paradigms for action and contemplation and, in doing so, directs our attention to the distinction our Lord makes between them: both are good, one is better. One is temporal and made of many parts; the other is one and integrates our entire life.

"Martha and Mary were two sisters by blood and by religion. Both cleaved to the Lord, both served the Lord with one heart while he was present in the flesh. Martha received him as a guest according to the usual custom. Yet the servant received her Lord, the sick her Savior, the creature her Creator. And she received him to feed him in the body while she was fed in the spirit.

"But let's get to the point proposed regarding unity. Martha, busy preparing and setting up to serve the Lord, was absorbed in her many services. Her sister, Mary, on the other hand, was being fed by the Lord. In a certain sense, she abandoned her sister to her many toils, and sat at the Lord's feet, hearing his Word in quiet.

"Martha was disturbed while Mary was feasting; one organizing many things, the other with her eyes on the One. Yet both tasks were good. But which one, should we say, was better? We have the One whom we may ask. Let's listen to him together.

"Martha appeals to her Guest, and places her reverent grievance before the Judge, claiming her sister abandoned her, and refused to help her when she was overwhelmed with serving. The Lord gave his judgment in front of Mary without any interjection from her. Mary, in her repose, deferred judgment to her Judge and chose not to answer. Indeed, if she were preparing a defense of words, she would have had to distract her earnest attention. Thus, the Lord, who found words no hurdle, since he was the Word, responded. With what? *Martha, Martha.* The repetition of the name is a sign of love, or perhaps as a way to get her attention, he says her name twice . . . *You busy yourself with so many things, but only one is necessary*, for the meaning of 'one thing' is not 'one work,' such as a single task, but one, needful, expedient, thing is necessary, and Martha has chosen it.

"Consider this 'one thing,' brethren, and see if anything pleases but this 'oneness,' even if amongst a multitude of things. Consider what a great number you are, thanks to God's mercy. But if you did not take care of this 'one thing,' who could put up with you? Why this silence if there are so many of you? Because where there is 'oneness,' there is a people. Take the 'oneness' away, and it becomes a throng.

"Thus, *Mary has chosen the better part, and it shall not be taken from her*. She chose what will last forever, 'and it shall not be taken from her.' She wanted to busy herself with 'one thing' . . . The Lord did not rebuke Martha's work; he simply distinguished between the two works. The work made up of any things is passing, the work made up of the 'one thing' abides forever. Labor shall be taken from you so you might rest, for you are still out on the sea. Mary, though, has already made it to port."[293]

Chapter 24

Progress in Prayer

90. Will my prayer always be the same?

Not if you persevere: "The very effort involved in prayer calms and purifies our heart, and makes it more capacious for receiving the divine gifts, which are poured into us spiritually. For it is not on account of the urgency of our prayers that God hears us, who is always ready to give us his light, not of a material kind, but that which is intellectual and spiritual: but we are not always ready to receive, since we are inclined toward other things, and are involved in darkness through our desire for temporal things. Hence there is brought about in prayer a turning of the heart to him, who is ever ready to give, if we will but take what he has given; and in the very act of turning there is effected a purging of the inner eye, inasmuch as those things of a temporal kind which were desired are excluded, so that the vision of the pure heart may be able to bear the pure light, divinely shining, without any setting or change: and not only to bear it, but also to remain in it; not merely without annoyance, but also with ineffable joy, in which a life truly and sincerely blessed is perfected."[294]

Note the steps of progress in the spiritual life according to this:

- "Turning of the heart to him" — conversion;
- "Purging of the inner eye" — purification of beginners;

- "Entrance into illumination" — proficiency: beginning to see the light with new vision;
- "Remaining in the light with joy" — perfection.

91. But doesn't this complicate things? If our prayer life is a relationship with Someone, why does Augustine treat it like a process or a system?

"Prayer is an affectionate turning of the mind toward God."[295] The way Augustine describes prayer, it seems to be less formal and much more relational. Of course, this personal relationship is imperfect unless there is a common ground of understanding — some identity of thought and interests. We should keep in mind that although the reason is involved, it has mostly to do with the will and growth in familiarity with God.

As in every relationship, there are two agents to be taken into account. Unless the soul desires to enter into dialog with God, there will be no prayer, and the soul cannot desire it unless God has made his presence felt in some way. God is the prime mover of all prayer, prompting our first desires to enter into a relationship with him. He sends us his Spirit to influence our intellects, to awaken the good that is in our memory, to arouse fervent desire to communicate with him. But God's desire for communication with each soul is intensely stronger than any desire we could muster or he could arouse in us. Although it is God's initiative, he does not exclude the free participation of the person he loves. As in any relationship, mutual cooperation is imperative. To progress in it, our task is first to ask him for his grace, and then act.

Rather than a dry or formal process, or even an activity carried out at a given time, prayer is a relationship which requires that we continually, as Augustine says, "turn our minds toward God." To be a contemplative is to have a habitual attitude of prayer.

92. What does this "turning the heart to him" look like practically? A simple act of the will?

Turning of the heart to him: On the one hand, we can say that the whole process is a turning of the heart to him. Further, the act of turning toward him effects an immediate commencement of the purification process: "Between baptism and eternal life there is time for prayer and remission of sins,[296] so as not to be overwhelmed by evil,[297] to attain a good will,[298] courage to live up to being a Christian.[299] Most certainly, it is the time to confess what one is and to pray to become what one is not."[300]

93. Isn't prayer's purging of the inner eye denigrating of the human person?

Purging the inner eye: by way of exercise of faith, hope, and charity, the Christian works toward his goal praying for the necessary grace to conform himself with his divine Ideal. Since "God expects of us to pray to him that he perfect us,"[301] this stage of spiritual growth is marked by a "purity of heart that urges us on to pray."[302] This "pure prayer," in turn, "purifies the way upon which we tend toward perfection."[303] In other words, our prayer spurs us on to a greater purity of heart, and this new spiritual state longs for a more profound prayer life. Such purity of heart makes us transparent in our dealings with God and his will, because in the depths of the pure heart there is total openness to the love of God and all that he loves. Thus, it is a virtuous circle.

But purity of heart is not attained without some suffering. For what is suffering? A longing for something I do not or cannot have. Augustine has told us how restless the heart is that does not rest in God, and this is so because the heart is so full of things that are not God. To get rid of those lower loves (Augustine calls them "burdens of dust and the mire of the world"[304]) in order to possess totally him who is Love, the person must suffer many deaths. And it is precisely this that has given many people the impression that following Christ is about mere self-denial and that somehow we miss out on what life wants to offer us. Hesitating to unburden ourselves of these burdens impedes our elevation to God. It is a refusal to "die a gospel death in order to live a gospel life. But once we have had success in this, we sense an immediate interior approval, 'Well done, well done!' not from men . . . but in a certain interior silence from which, I know not where, arises that sound, 'Well done, well done!' "[305]

94. What does one have to do to enter into illumination?

Entrance into illumination: With a renewed and purified interior vision, directly helped from on high, the soul begins to see new realities and old ones in a new light. The intellect is more receptive to the divine truths which are no longer theory, but a lived reality, almost tangible. This affects the prayer life substantially, which has passed from vocal prayer to meditation. The soul in this stage is completely oriented "toward the highest and most secret reward, in order to achieve that for which it has fought so hard."[306]

Nonetheless, the path of illumination, for all of its consolation and sweetness, does not exclude suffering and purgation. "What has happened to me is quite strange, but true; I lament because I am deprived of your vision, and yet my grief comforts me . . . Do we not long for the heavenly Jerusalem? And the more impatiently we long for it, do we not the more patiently suffer all things for its sake?"[307] So grieved is the soul in love with God in its exile, that such sorrow is compared to an interior wound: "The wound of love is a wound that heals. In the Song of Songs the spouse of Christ sings, *I am wounded with love* (5:8). And this wound, when will it be healed? When our desire is satisfied in good things. As long as what we do not possess what we long for, it is called a wound. When we come to possess what we desire then the pain passes, but the love will never pass."[308]

But that is not all. Concomitant with this interior trial, God blesses the generous soul with exterior trials, often under the guise of calumny, persecution, and loss. "When a Christian begins to consider spiritual progress, he begins to suffer from the tongues of his adversaries. He, on the other hand, who has not yet suffered from such as these, has made no progress. And he who does not suffer these things, does not attempt to advance. Does he want to understand what I mean with this? Experience a bit of what we are compelled to listen to. Then try to advance, to even desire to advance, to despise earthly, perishable, temporal things, and hold this world's happiness as empty, thinking of God alone, never rejoicing in gain or lamenting loss, desiring to sell all he owns and give it to the poor in order to follow Christ. Then let's see how he suffers the tongues of calumniators and many other things from his enemies and, what is more, the attempts of false advisors who would lead him away from salvation."[309]

95. They say nobody's perfect. So how can prayer really lead us to perfection?

Remaining in the light with joy: this is the soul that has reached perfection — attainable even in this life. In this state, the person's prayer becomes passive, for it is more *the Holy Spirit who prays* in him than his own effort. He has reached contemplation. Such a person has identified his will and affections with God's, and "by grace already observes a perpetual Sabbath rest, who carries out every work in view of a future rest, and does not glory in his own works as if he had anything good that he had not first received . . . *now he walks in the newness of life* (Rom. 6:4), he recognizes God working in him, who both works and rests, both controlling and projecting his creation; and finding in God his eternal rest."[310] "And that very joy in the tranquility of our hope is our Sabbath."[311]

"For this contemplation is promised to us as the end of all actions and the eternal consummation of all joys . . . For that which he said to Moses his servant: *I AM WHO AM* . . . This is what we shall contemplate when we shall live eternally . . . For contemplation is the reward of faith, for which reward our hearts are cleansed by faith."[312]

Nonetheless, Augustine does not reduce spiritual perfection to some sort of passive complacency. To the contrary, he reduces it to the perfection of love, divine charity, God's presence reigning in our hearts. "This is true love: that we cling to the truth and live righteously."[313] Charity as the norm for Christian perfection is the full living out of the first gift of the Holy Spirit.[314] This is the good which makes the possession of all other goods possible, and whose absence makes all other goods impossible: "Have charity and you will have them all; because without charity, whatever you have will be of no benefit."[315] This is so, because it is the essence of every other virtue. Only well-ordered love makes the other virtues possible.[316] In other words, the difference between mere human values (which are not enough for salvation or holiness) and Christianity is their source. "From where does love for God and neighbor come if not from God himself?"[317]

96. But I haven't made it yet. I'm far from perfect and I can't see myself making it in this life. What am I to do?

Don't worry. St. Augustine says, "Recognizing your own imperfection is part of achieving perfection"![318] He would also doubtlessly counsel you to keep your focus on Christ and not so much on yourself. How do you do that? Desire. "*As a doe longs for running streams, so longs my soul for you, my God*. Who is it that says this? We do, if we would only will it! And why ask who it might be, as if it could be anybody other than yourself, since it is in your power to be the very thing about which you inquire? It is not merely one individual, but rather it is 'one Body' and 'Christ's Body is the Church.' This longing is not found in everyone who enters the Church: let all who have tasted the sweetness of the Lord, and who have developed a relish for Christ, let them know that there are many such seeds scattered throughout the field of the Lord, which is the earth."[319]

The good news for the downcast soul who recognizes her own weakness and deficiencies in the spiritual life is that, as a member of the Mystical Body that is the Church, she can join her weak desire for Christ to the perfect nuptial desire for Christ that proceeds from the Church and participate in it.

"Certainly, it is not hard to understand as are those cries of the catechumens who hurry to the grace of the holy [baptismal] font. But indeed this psalm is normally sung on such occasions, so that they will long for the font of remission of sins, just as the *doe longs for running streams* . . . Nonetheless, it seems to me that this 'longing' is not fully satisfied even in the faithful who are baptized; rather, if they understand to where they journey and from where they have come, their 'longing' is enkindled to an even greater intensity."[320]

Augustine is saying that what Baptism has obtained for the soul and makes possible to obtain is dependent on one's desire for such goods. Such desire which achieves absolute possession is only possible in eternity. Augustine's mysticism of desiring to assimilate and internalize everything that pertains to Baptism is within everyone's grasp, and is simply a question of cooperating with God's grace and firm, constant exercise of the will in the form of desire.

And if our desire should falter, we should unite ourselves to the Church's pure desire for Christ and benefit from her merits.

So long as we are in this life, we must manage our imperfect state. "We will not enjoy perfect health if we do not have perfect charity . . . but we will have perfect charity when we see God as he is. And then there will be nothing more to add to our love when we are blessed with that vision."[321]

Thus, our perfection in this life is relative. "Always be discontent with your [spiritual] state if you want to arrive at perfection. Because when you content yourself with yourself, you cease to progress. If you were to say, 'That's enough. I have arrived at perfection,' you will have lost everything."[322]

Augustine does not make spiritual perfection other-worldly; rather, he says, "It can be held, without fear of falling into absurdity, that to advance faultlessly is possible for the imperfect, if he runs toward perfection, avoiding the capital sins and not omitting to purify himself of venial sins by means of almsgiving."[323]

Further, he says, "The more you love, the more you are elevated."[324] And elsewhere he says, "Where love grows, concupiscence diminishes."[325]

Chapter 25

Fine-Tuning and Miscellaneous Questions on Prayer

97. Does it matter what posture I adopt in prayer?

More than a physical position, St. Augustine insists on an interior disposition when approaching prayer. Bishop Simplitianus asked Augustine what to make of the line in Sacred Scripture, *King David entered and sat before the Lord* (2 Kings 7:18). In his response, Augustine distinguishes between two "moments" that the life of prayer offers us:

• *When we seek our Lord in prayer:* in this case we should adopt the posture that most helps our interior to seek and find God. Each one of us knows what works best, and we should keep to that.

• *When our Lord seeks us in prayer:* in this case, God will find us regardless of our posture, and it will not matter if we are seated, standing, kneeling, prostrate, or walking. He says that in such cases, we should not wait for a better moment or put off such communion with God for any reason. If God knocks at the door of our heart, we should open immediately.[326]

In another passage, he says that, "the intention of the spirit generates solitude,"[327] which means that the best condition for good prayer, beyond posture, time of day, and place, is our own interior disposition. After God's grace, nothing is more important than our attitude, which is a reflection of our desire. Often we do not control the time and place of our prayer, but our interior posture is something over which we have complete control.

98. What if I feel unworthy of entering into communion with God? Intimacy with the Almighty seems so presumptuous.

If that's how you feel, then you qualify to have a very intimate relationship with God. Proud people can have no communion with him, but God can lead a humble soul who recognizes his own sinfulness to the heights of sanctity. Just read St. Augustine's *Confessions* to see what God can do with anyone who is willing to admit his own unworthiness. God does not seek our righteousness, but our hearts. Once we have given him our hearts, he can give us a share in his righteousness. "He dwells on high, but has regard for the lowly. *The Lord is near.* To whom? To the high, perhaps? No, *to the contrite of heart* . . . It is a wonderful thing: he dwells on high, and yet is near to the lowly; 'he has regard for lowly things, but lofty things he knows from afar'; he sees the proud from afar, and the higher they appear to be to themselves, the farther he is from them."[328]

99. We have spoken a lot about asking God for things in prayer. Does he ask us anything in prayer?

In a somewhat roundabout way St. Augustine says that God asks us to imitate his magnanimity.

"We have spoken about who it is from whom we ask things, and who we are that ask, as well as about what we should ask for. But we are called upon, too, for we are God's beggars. So that he may acknowledge us as his mendicants, let us, for our part, acknowledge our own status as beggars. Consider once again the case in which something is asked of us: who they are that ask, from whom do they ask, and what do they ask for? Who, then, are they that ask us? Men. From whom do they ask? From men. Who ask? Mortals. To whom do they beg? Mortals. Aside from the matter of wealth, the beggars are just like those who are asked. With what nerve can you beg the Lord, you who do not acknowledge your equal? 'I am not,' he will respond, 'like him.' So it is that one who is dressed in silk and filled up with pride speaks about one dressed in rags. But I put it to you, when you are both stripped, are you not as you are now, but as you were when you were born? Both were crying because you were naked, weak, and beginning a life of suffering."[329]

100. What does Augustine say about the mystical experience?

"Spiritually to touch God a little is a great joy; but to grasp him is entirely impossible."[330] Augustine is saying that God can be experienced but is beyond every type of human experience. This prohibits us from reifying God or trying to shoehorn him into our limited thoughts, for he is everywhere and the All; he contains everything and nothing contains him.[331] And he goes on to say that "it is better to find God without understanding him, than to understand him without finding him."[332]

This inability to express his experience of God can be called a "learned ignorance — an ignorance learned from God's Spirit, who assists us in our weakness."[333]

His experience of God, as is common to the mystical experience, transcended human concepts; thus, he was forced to describe the mystical experience as a "feeling" God brings about in man by divine Love.[334] And experiencing God's love brings man to participate in it, which, in turn makes us similar to God.

"Look on all that is created, admire it all, but seek its Maker. If you are dissimilar to him, you will turn away from him. If you are like him, you will rejoice. And if you are like him and begin to approach, you will feel God, and his love will increase in you, since God is love. Then you will perceive, if only partially, what you cannot express. Before you felt God, you thought you could express God. Once you begin to feel him, you feel that what is felt is inexpressible."[335]

The closer one comes to God, the more one feels him; the more one feels God, the more one loves him; and this continual growth in love for God is what makes a person similar to God. Nonetheless, the lived experience of God will always escape human words. Far from being a problem, for Augustine, this inexpressibility is a sign of authenticity.

"Let us search for that which should be found, and go into that which has already been discovered. The One we need to find has been hidden so that we seek him. But once found, he is found to be infinite so that he continues to be the object of our search. Therefore, it says elsewhere, *Seek his face evermore*. He satisfies the seeker completely and makes the discoverer capable of even more, that he be filled anew according to the proportion of his ability to receive. In this sense, *seek his face evermore* is not said in the sense of those who are *always learning and never coming to knowledge of the truth* (2 Tim. 3:7); but rather as the preacher says, *When a man has finished, then he begins* (Ecclus. 18:5), until we reach that life where we, too, shall be filled and our natures achieve their utmost capacity, because then we will have arrived at perfection and need not seek more. But so long as we are here, we seek and our rewarded discovery will not bring an end to our search."[336]

Chapter 26

The Beginning

101. Will our prayer finally come to an end in heaven?

At the end of our earthly life and entering into heaven, our prayer life takes a new form. It begins to flourish in ways it never could in this life. Augustine makes our primary occupation in heaven to be prayer — but prayer in the form of singing God's praise with an everlasting *Alleluia*. "*Alleluia* is praise of God. To us, as we labor, it means the act of resting. For when we come to our rest after those labors, God's praise will be our sole occupation, for there our task will be *Alleluia* . . . Some sweet odor of divine praise and that of rest reaches us, but for the greater part, it is our mortality that weighs upon us. But we grow weary of saying it and desire to exercise our limbs. And if we say *Alleluia* for too long, God's praise itself becomes onerous, thanks to this mass of flesh that we are. For once the labors of this life and this world itself ceases, there will be an unceasing fullness in *Alleluia* . . . We must say it as often as we can. Let us deserve to say it forever! For there our food will be *Alleluia*, our drink will be *Alleluia*, the object of our rest will be *Alleluia*, all our joy will be *Alleluia*; that is, God's praise . . . What strength there will be in the mind, what immortality and endurance in the body, that neither the mind shall tire, nor the limbs grow weary under the everlasting praise of God!"[337]

End Notes

[1] *Sermon* 117, 5.
[2] *Sermon* 1, 6, 10.
[3] *Sermon* 47, 14, 23.
[4] *Confessions*, 10, 27, 38.
[5] *Commentary on Sermon on the Mount*, 2, 5, 14.
[6] *Exposition on Psalms (Expo. Ps.)*, 65, 20.
[7] *Sermon* 210, 7, 8.
[8] *Sermon* 159, 1.
[9] *Sermon* 210, 9.
[10] *Sermon* 56, 2, 2.
[11] *Sermon* 83, 2, 2.
[12] *Commentary on John's Gospel (Comm. Jn.)*, 102, 3.
[13] *Letter* 130, 8, 17.
[14] *Expo. Ps.* 37, 12.
[15] *Expo. Ps.* 130, 24.
[16] *Expo. Ps.* 141, 1.
[17] *Expo. Ps.* 85, 10.
[18] *Comm. Jn.*, 26, 2.
[19] *Expo. Ps.* 91, 8.
[20] *Expo. Ps.* 114, 6.
[21] *Confessions*, 7, 10, 16.
[22] Ibid.
[23] Ibid., 1, 4.
[24] Ibid., 6, 3, 3.
[25] Ibid., 3, 6, 11.
[26] Ibid., 11, 4, 10.
[27] *On Genesis*, 8, 26, 48.
[28] *Confessions*, 10, 27, 38.
[29] *Expo. Ps.* 141, 2.
[30] *Expo. Ps.* 33, 2, 8.
[31] *Sermon* 96, 2, 2.
[32] *Confessions*, 5, 2, 2.
[33] Ibid. 7, 10, 16.
[34] *Comm. Jn.*, 15, 24, 5.
[35] *On Christian Doctrine*, 4, 30, 63.
[36] *Sermon* 210, 9.
[37] *Sermon* 153, 8.
[38] Cf. *Expo. Ps.* 80, 2.
[39] *Expo. Ps.* 62, 7, 13.
[40] Cf. *Confessions*, 4, 5, 10.
[41] Cf. *Expo. Ps.* 65, 20.
[42] *Expo. Ps.* 61, 3.

[43] *Sermon* 47, 14, 23.
[44] *Confessions*, 1, 1, 1.
[45] *Sermon* 47, 14, 23.
[46] *Comm. Jn.*, 17, 11.
[47] Ibid., 10, 1.
[48] *On the True Religion*, 39, 72.
[49] *The Teacher*, 11, 38.
[50] *Confessions*, 5, 2, 2.
[51] *Confessions*, 9, 4, 10.
[52] Ibid., 1, 4, 4.
[53] Ibid., 3, 6, 11.
[54] Ibid., 10, 27, 38.
[55] *On the True Religion*, 39, 72.
[56] *The Teacher*, 11, 38.
[57] *Confessions*, 1, 1, 1.
[58] *On the Trinity*, 14, 8, 11.
[59] Ibid., 14, 14, 6.
[60] *On the City of God*, 12, 3, 3.
[61] *On the Trinity*, 14, 8, 11.
[62] *Letter* 130, 1, 2.
[63] *Expo. Ps.* 15, 9.
[64] *On the Trinity*, 15, 1, 2.
[65] Ibid.
[66] *Expo. Ps.* 129, 1.
[67] *Sermon* 1, 10.
[68] *Expo. Ps.* 106, 4-6; 11.
[69] *Expo. Ps.* 50, 25.
[70] *Against Julian*, 6, 15.
[71] *On Nature and Grace*, 43, 50; 69, 83.
[72] *Letter* 187, 27.
[73] *Expo. Ps.* 116, 8, 10.
[74] *On Nature and Grace*, 26, 29.
[75] *Letter* 187, 27.
[76] *On the Gift of Perseverance*, 16, 29.
[77] *On Grace and Free Choice*, 16, 32.
[78] Ibid., 26, 29.
[79] *On Nature and Grace*, 43, 50.
[80] *Confessions*, 10, 29, 40.
[81] *On Merit and Remission of Sin*, 2, 5, 5.
[82] *On Letter and the Spirit*, 19, 34.
[83] *Against Julian*, 6, 15.
[84] *Letter* 130, 29.
[85] *Letter* 20, 2.
[86] *Confessions*, 10, 22.
[87] *Letter* 149, 2, 17.
[88] *Sermon* 110, 1.
[89] *Comm. Jn.*, 58, 5.
[90] *On the Gift of Perseverance*, 22, 60.
[91] *Letter* 111, 8.
[92] *Comm. Jn.*, 1, 8.
[93] *On the Gift of Perseverance*, 20, 60.
[94] Ibid., 6, 15.
[95] *Letter* 231.
[97] *Expo. Ps.* 85, 2.
[98] *Letter* 130, 24.
[99] *The City of God*, 10, 6.
[100] *Sermon* 115, 1.
[101] *Confessions*, 13, 9.
[102] Ibid.
[103] Ibid.

[104] *On the Letter of John*, 6, 4.
[105] *Homilies on the Sermon on the Mount*, 2, 3, 13.
[106] *Tract. on John*, 86, 3.
[107] *Letter* 130, 9, 18.
[108] *Rule*, 10.
[109] *Expo. Ps.* 49, 23.
[110] *Letter* 9, 1.
[111] *Sacrosanctum Concilium*, 10, 14.
[112] *Letter* 55, 18, 34.
[113] *Confessions*, 9, 6, 14.
[114] Ibid., 10, 33, 50.
[115] *Expo. Ps.* 32, 1, 8.
[116] *Sermon* 336, 1, 1.
[117] No. 13.
[118] *Expo. Ps.* 144, 2.
[119] Ibid., 4.
[120] *Expo. Ps.* 37, 14.
[121] *Confessions* 1, 1.
[122] *Retractions*, 2, 6, 1.
[123] *Expo. Ps.* 44, 9.
[124] Ibid., 72, 37.
[125] Ibid., 88, 8.
[126] *Expo. Ps.* 104, 1; *Sermon* 183, 5.
[127] Expo. *Ps.* 45, 8.
[128] *Expo. Ps.* 146, 2-3.
[129] *Expo. Ps.* 144, 4.
[130] *Confessions*, 12, 11, 11.
[131] Ibid., 12, 11, 12.
[132] *City of God*, 10, 6.
[133] *Expo. Ps.* 98, 9.
[134] *City of God*, 22, 30.
[135] *Confessions*, 2, 7, 5.
[136] *Letter* 41, 1.
[137] *Expo. Ps.* 102, 11.
[138] Ibid., 44, 18.
[139] Ibid.. 58, 1, 13.
[140] Ibid., 85, 1.
[141] *City of God*, 10, 16.
[142] *Expo. Ps.* 85, 8.
[143] *On the Forgiveness of Sins*, 3, 13, 23.
[144] *On Grace*, 11, 26; 12, 27.
[145] *Expo. Ps.* 31, 17.
[146] Cf. *Homily* 47, 7.
[147] *Expo. Ps.* 101, 10.
[148] Ibid., 79, 2.
[149] *Letter* 130, 17.
[150] *Letter* 21.
[151] *Sermon* 61, 1, 3.
[152] Ibid., 61, 4.
[153] Ibid., 61, 5, 6.
[154] *On the Gift of Perseverance*, 16, 39.
[155] *Letter* 130, 31.
[156] *Incomplete Work Against Julian*, 6, 15.
[157] *Letter* 130, 16, 29.
[159] *Expo. Ps.* 33, 2.
[160] *Expo. Ps.* 12, 23.
[161] Ibid., 12, 22.
[162] Ibid., 11, 21.
[163] Ibid., 12, 22.
[164] *Letter* 130, 13.
[165] *Letter* 22, 1.

[166] *On Christian Doctrine*, 4, 15, 32; 16, 33; 17, 34.
[167] *On Admonition and Grace*, 6, 10.
[168] *On Nature and Grace*, 68, 82.
[169] Ibid., 11, 21.
[170] *Expo. Ps.* 147, 1.
[171] *Letter* 199, 5, 15.
[172] *Letter* 12, 22.
[173] *Sermon* 80, 2.
[174] *Sermon* 68, 82.
[175] *Letter* 130, 16.
[176] *On Nature and Grace*, 16, 17.
[177] *On Sin*, 3, 2, 4.
[178] *On the Soul and Its Origin*, 4, 9, 13.
[179] *Expo. Ps.* 145, 6.
[180] Ibid., 118, 14, 2.
[181] *Letter* 194, 4, 18; 217, 7, 28; *On the Blessed Life*, 17, 21.
[182] *Letter* 130, 11, 21.
[183] Ibid., 12, 22.
[184] *Expo. Ps.* 32, 56.
[185] *Expo. Ps.* 119, 14.
[186] *Sermon* 384, 4.
[187] *Expo. Ps.* 118.
[188] *Sermon* 154.
[189] *Letter* 130, 11, 21.
[190] Ibid., 12, 22.
[191] Ibid., 9.
[192] *Sermon* 56, 2, 2.
[193] *On Christian Doctrine*, 3, 37, 6.
[194] *Sermon* 80, 7.
[195] *Letter* 130, 11, 21.
[196] Ibid., 2, 22.
[197] *On Adulterous Marriages*, 2, 13, 13.
[198] *The City of God*, 5, 24.
[199] *On Nature and Grace*, 34, 41.
[200] *Expo. Ps.* 70, 3.
[201] *Sermon* 105, A/2.
[202] *On Nature and Grace*, 68, 82.
[203] *Sermon* 47, 5, 6.
[204] *Non est miser, sed misericors; Homily* 259, 3.
[205] *Letter* 130, 11, 21.
[206] Ibid., 12, 22.
[207] *Expo. Ps.* 45, 4.
[208] *On Sin*, 2, 6, 7.
[209] *On Continence*, 5, 13.
[210] *Confessions*, 10, 30, 42.
[211] *Expo. Ps.* 60, 2.
[212] *Letter* 130, 11, 21.
[213] Ibid., 12, 22.
[214] *On Merit and Remission of Sin*, 2, 19, 33.
[215] *On Admonition and Grace*, 34, 41.
[216] *Expo Ps.* 51, 8; 55, 12; 61, 23; *Letter* 264, 2.
[217] *Expo. Ps.* 51, 8.
[218] *On Admonition and Grace*, 5, 8.
[219] *On Nature and Grace*, 65, 68.
[220] *Expo. Ps.* 70, 3.
[221] *Sermon* 151, 4.

[222] *Comm. Jn.*, 73, 1.
[223] *On Nature and Grace*, 66, 79.
[224] *Letter* 130, 14, 25.
[225] Ibid., 27.
[226] *Expo. Ps.* 45, 8.
[227] *Letter* 130, 5, 11.
[228] Ibid., 16, 29.
[229] Ibid., 16, 30.
[230] Ibid., 6, 12.
[231] *Expo. Ps.* 186, 7.
[232] Ibid.
[233] Ibid.
[234] *Comm. Jn.*, 73, 1.
[235] *Sermon* 77/B, 3.
[236] *Expo. Ps.* 80, 7.
[237] Ibid., 22, 4.
[238] Ibid., 144, 19.
[239] Ibid., 36, 9.
[240] *Comm. Jn.*, 86, 3.
[241] *Letter* 130, 6, 12.
[242] *Expo. Ps.* 103, 1, 3.
[243] *Comm. Jn.*, 102, 2.
[244] *Sermon* 80, 2.
[245] *Letter* 130, 23.
[246] *Sermon* 105/A, 2; *Letter* 130, 23.
[247] *Commentary on Romans*, 64.
[248] *Expo. Ps.* 21, 8.
[249] Ibid., 144, 19.
[250] *Comm. Jn.*, 73, 4.
[251] *Sermon* 61/A, 5.
[252] *Letter* 130, 12, 23.
[253] *Expo. Ps.* 33, 2.
[254] Ibid., 33, 4.
[255] Ibid., 146, 2.
[256] *Sermon* 105, 1, 1.
[257] *Expo. Ps.* 83, 6.
[258] *On the Gift of Perseverance*, 24, 66.
[259] *Expo. Ps.* 144, 19.
[260] *Letter* 130, 10, 19.
[261] Ibid.
[262] Ibid., 10, 20.
[263] Ibid., 9, 18.
[264] *Expo. Ps.* 102, 9.
[265] Ibid., 62, 5.
[266] *Comm. Jn.*, 41, 10.
[267] *City of God*, 6, 9, 5.
[268] *Expo. Ps.* 102, 9.
[269] *Sermon* 61, 6.
[270] *Expo. Ps.* 39, 3.
[271] *Letter* 130, 5.
[272] *Against the Heretics*, 57.
[273] *Sermon* 77/B, 1.
[274] *Expo. Ps.* 118, 29.
[275] *Letter* 149, 2, 16.
[276] *On Merit and the Remission of Sin*, 2, 26, 42.
[277] *Sermon* 205, 2.
[278] *Expo. Ps.* 86, 1.
[279] Ibid.
[280] Ibid., 86, 5.
[281] *Expo. Ps.* 131, 1.
[282] Ibid., 2.
[283] *Expo. Ps.* 144, 1.
[284] Ibid., 2.

[285] *Commentary on the First Letter of John*, 1, 8.
[286] *Tract. on John*, 1, 4.
[287] Ibid., 81, 4.
[288] *Soliloquies*, 1, 1, 5.
[289] *Letter* 48, 1.
[290] *City of God*, 19, 19.
[291] Ibid.
[292] *On the Harmony of the Gospels*, 1, 5, 8.
[293] *Sermon* 53, 2, 3, 4; *Sermon* 54, 3.
[294] *Sermon on the Mount*, 2, 3, 14.
[295] *Sermon* 11, 3.
[296] *On the Proceedings Against Pelagius*, 12, 28.
[297] Ibid., 14, 31.
[298] *Sermon* 105/A, 2.
[299] *Expo. Ps.* 68, 2, 4.
[300] Ibid., 105, 7.
[301] Ibid., 85, 7.
[302] Ibid., 33, 2, 8.
[303] *On the Perfection of Man*, 8, 19.
[304] *Letter* 95, 112.
[305] Ibid.
[306] *On the Greatness of the Soul*, 33, 74.
[307] *Letter* 27, 1.
[308] *Sermon* 298, 2, 2.
[309] *Expo. Ps.* 119, 3.
[310] *On Genesis*, 4, 13, 221.
[311] *Expo. Ps.* 90, 2.
[312] *On the Trinity*, 1, 8, 17.
[313] *On Catechizing the Unlearned*, 1, 8.
[314] *Comm. Jn.*, 87, 1.
[315] Ibid. 32, 8.
[316] *The City of God*, 2, 22.
[317] *On Grace and Free Choice*, 18, 37.
[318] *On Perfect Justice of Man*, 10, 20.
[319] *Expo. Ps.* 42, 1.
[320] Ibid.
[321] *On the Perfect Justice of Man*, 3, 8.
[322] *Sermon* 169, 18.
[323] *On the Perfect Justice of Man*, 10, 20.
[324] *Expo. Ps.* 83, 10.
[325] *Ench.* 121, 32.
[326] *Various Questions asked by Simplitianus*, 2, question 4.
[327] *Tract. on John*, 17, 11.
[328] Ibid., 15, 24, 5.
[329] *Sermon* 61, 8.
[330] *Sermon* 117, 5.
[331] *Confessions*, 1, 3, 3.
[332] Ibid., 1, 6, 10.
[333] *Letter* 130, 28.
[334] *Expo. Ps.* 99, 5.
[335] Ibid., 6.
[336] *Tract. on John*, 63, 1.
[337] *Sermon* 252, 9, 9.

Bibliography

INTRODUCTION

Cary, Phillip. *Augustine: Philosopher and Saint.* Audio-course published by The Teaching Company, Chantilly, Virginia, 1997.

———. *Inner Grace.* New York: Oxford University Press, 2008.

———. *Outward Signs.* New York: Oxford University Press, 2008.

Eslin, Jean-Claude. *Saint Augustin: L'homme occidental.* Paris: Michalon, 2002.

Harrison, Carol. Augustine: *Christian Truth and Fractured Humanity.* New York: Oxford University Press, 2000.

Marshall, Michael. *The Restless Heart: The Life and Influence of St. Augustine*, Eerdmans, Grand Rapids, 1987.

CORPUS OF THE BOOK

Augustinus Aurelius Hipponensis episcopus. *Opera Omnia (multis sermonibus ineditis aucta et locupletata).* Vol. 1-42. Paris: Accurantibus A. B. Caillau [et] M.N.S. Guillon, Apud Parent-Desbarres, 1760-1847. Latin texts used for this translation.

Burnaby, John. *Amor Dei: A Study of the Religion of Saint Augustine*. London: Hodder and Stoughton, 1938.

Butler, Cuthbert. *Western Mysticism*. 3rd ed. London, 1951.

Dotto, Giovanni. *Conoscere e amare: l'Amore nei libri 8. e 9. de "La Trinità" / Sant'Agostino*. Rome: Nuova Biblioteca Agostiniana, 1991.

Madec, Goulvan. *La bibliotèque augustinienne / présentation d'ensemble, tables analytique des introductions et des notes complementaires*. Paris: Études Augustiniennes, 1988.

Mandouze, Andre. *Saint Augustin: L'Aventure de raison et de grace*. Paris: Études Augustiniennes, 1968.

Margerie, Bertrand de. *Introduction à l'histoire de l'exégèse: III, Saint Augustin*. Paris: Cerf, 1983.

Portalie, Eugene. *A Guide to the Thought of Saint Augustine*. Chicago: Regnery, 1960.

Rossellini, Roberto. *Sant'Agostino*. Rome: R.A.I., 1972.

Santi, Giorgio. *I Soliloqui*. Rome: Città Nuova, 1997.

Trapè, Agostino. *Il sacerdote uomo di Dio e servo della Chiesa*. Milan: Editrice Ancora, 1968.

———. *Introduzione Generale a San Agostino*. Rome: Nuova Biblioteca Agostiniana, 1987.

———. *La nozione del mutabile e dell'immutabile secondo Sant'Agostino*. Tolentino: Convento San Nicola, 1959.

———. *La presenza di Dio: lettera a Dardano di Sant'Agostino*. *Rome: Città Nuova, 2006.*

———. *Le Esposizioni di S. Agostino sui Salmi: Divinitas* 22. Rome, 1978.

———. *Lettera apostolica "Agustino d'Ippona" nel XVI centenario della conversione di S. Agostino: commento*. Rome: Nuova Biblioteca Agostiniana, 1988.

———. *Opere di Sant'Agostino — Introduzione Generale*. Rome: Città Nuova, 2006.

———. *S. Agostino. L'uomo, il pastore, il mistico*. Fossano: Editrice Esperienze, 1976.

———. *Sant'Agostino. La preghiera: Lettera a Proba e Commento al Padre Nostro*. Rome: Piccola Biblioteca Agostiniana, 1995.

———. *Sant'Agostino: Il Maestro Interiore — testi scelti, introduzione e commenti*. Milan: Edizione Paoline, 1987.

About the Author and the Editor

St. Augustine was the Bishop of Hippo in North Africa during the late fourth century and early fifth. He is one of the best known and best loved of the Church Fathers, and his prolific writings have dominated Western thought and are still an inspiration today — not least to Pope Benedict XVI. Augustine had the gift of writing vividly and with a love for his readers that shone through the prose of his letters and homilies. Aside from his important work in philosophy and theology, he was a true shepherd of souls and a guide to the spiritual life.

Augustine is famous above all for two of the great classics of Christian literature: the *Confessions*, about his own spiritual journey toward God, and *The City of God*, which contains a theological vision of history.

∞

Fr. Cliff Ermatinger is a Chicago native and works as a parish priest in the Archdiocese of Chicago. Along with this first book for Sophia Institute Press, he also wrote *Common Nonsense: 25 Fallacies about Life . . . Refuted*.

Sophia Institute Press®

Sophia Institute is a nonprofit institution that seeks to restore man's knowledge of eternal truth, including man's knowledge of his own nature, his relation to other persons, and his relation to God. Sophia Institute Press® serves this end in numerous ways: it publishes translations of foreign works to make them accessible for the first time to English-speaking readers; it brings out-of-print books back into print; and it publishes important new books that fulfill the ideals of Sophia Institute. These books afford readers a rich source of the enduring wisdom of mankind.

Sophia Institute Press® makes these high-quality books available to the general public by using advanced technology and by soliciting donations to subsidize its general publishing costs. Your generosity can help Sophia Institute Press® to provide the public with editions of works containing the enduring wisdom of the ages. Please send your tax-deductible contribution to the address below. We welcome your questions, comments, and suggestions.

For your free catalog, call:

Toll-free: 1-800-888-9344

Sophia Institute Press®
Box 5284 • Manchester, NH • 03108
www.sophiainstitute.com